★ OLYMPIC GUIDES ★

A BASIC GUIDE TO

Speed Skating

An Official U.S. Olympic Committee Sports Series

The U.S. Olympic Committee

Griffin Publishing Group

ISBN 1-58000-087-8

10 9 8 7 6 5 4 3 2 1

Editorial Statement
In the interest of brevity, the Editors have chosen to use the standard English form of address. Please be advised that this usage is not meant to suggest a restriction to, nor an endorsement of, any individual or group of individuals, either by age, gender, or athletic ability. The Editors certainly acknowledge that boys and girls, men and women, of every age and physical condition are actively involved in sports, and we encourage everyone to enjoy the sports of his or her choice.

Griffin Publishing Group
2908 Oregon Court, Suite I-5
Torrance, CA 90503
Tel: (310)381-0485 Fax: (310)381-0499

ACKNOWLEDGMENTS

PUBLISHER	Griffin Publishing Group
DIR. / OPERATIONS	Robin L. Howland
PROJECT MANAGER	Bryan K. Howland
WRITER	Cathy Breitenbucher
BOOK DESIGN	m2design group

US SPEEDSKATING PRESIDENT	Bill Cushman
EXECUTIVE DIRECTOR	Katie Marquard
EDITORS	Geoffrey M. Horn
	Laurie Gibson

PHOTOS	Photo Action USA
COVER DESIGN	m2design group
COVER PHOTO	Cy White/Photo Action USA
ATHLETE ON COVER	Bonnie Blair

Griffin Publishing Group would like to thank Cy White of Photo Action USA
for all of his help throughout the production of this book.

THE UNITED STATES OLYMPIC COMMITTEE

The U.S. Olympic Committee (USOC) is the custodian of the U.S. Olympic Movement and is dedicated to providing opportunities for American athletes of all ages.

The USOC, a streamlined organization of member organizations, is the moving force for support of sports in the United States that are on the program of the Olympic and/or Pan American Games, or those wishing to be included.

The USOC has been recognized by the International Olympic Committee since 1894 as the sole agency in the United States whose mission involves training, entering, and underwriting the full expenses for the United States teams in the Olympic and Pan American Games. The USOC also supports the bid of U.S. cities to host the winter and summer Olympic Games, or the winter and summer Pan American Games, and after reviewing all the candidates, votes on and may endorse one city per event as the U.S. bid city. The USOC also approves the U.S. trial sites for the Olympic and Pan American Games team selections.

WELCOME TO THE OLYMPIC SPORTS SERIES

We feel this unique series will encourage parents, athletes of all ages, and novices who are thinking about a sport for the first time to get involved with the challenging and rewarding world of Olympic sports.

This series of Olympic sport books covers both summer and winter sports, features Olympic history and basic sports fundamentals, and encourages family involvement. Each book includes information on how to get started in a particular sport, including equipment and clothing; rules of the game; health and fitness; basic first aid; and guidelines for spectators. Of special interest is the information on opportunities for senior citizens, volunteers, and physically challenged athletes. In addition, each book is enhanced by photographs and illustrations and a complete, easy-to-understand glossary.

Because this family-oriented series neither assumes nor requires prior knowledge of a particular sport, it can be enjoyed by all age groups. Regardless of anyone's level of sports knowledge, playing experience, or athletic ability, this official U.S. Olympic Committee Sports Series will encourage understanding and participation in sports and fitness.

The purchase of these books will assist the U.S. Olympic Team. This series supports the Olympic mission and serves importantly to enhance participation in the Olympic and Pan American Games.

United States Olympic Committee

Contents

AN ATHLETE'S CREED

The most important thing in the Olympic Games is not to win but to take part, just as the most important thing in life is not the triumph but the struggle. The essential thing is not to have conquered but to have fought well.

These famous words, commonly referred to as the Olympic Creed, were once spoken by Baron Pierre de Coubertin, founder of the modern Olympic Games. Whatever their origins, they aptly describe the theme behind each and every Olympic competition.

Metric Equivalents

Wherever possible, measurements given are those specified by the Olympic rules. Other measurements are given in metric or standard U.S. units, as appropriate. For purposes of comparison, the following rough equivalents may be used.

1 kilometer (km)	= 0.62 mile (mi)	1 mi = 1.61 km
1 meter (m)	= 3.28 feet (ft)	1 ft = 0.305 m
	= 1.09 yards (yd)	1 yd = 0.91 m
1 centimeter (cm)	= 0.39 inch (in)	1 in = 2.54 cm
	= 0.1 hand	1 hand (4 in) = 10.2 cm
1 kilogram (kg)	= 2.2 pounds (lb)	1 lb = 0.45 kg
1 milliliter (ml)	= 0.03 fluid ounce (fl oz)	1 fl oz = 29.573 ml
1 liter	= 0.26 gallons (gal)	1 gal = 3.785 liters

1

Speed Skating in Olympic History

Speed skating is one of the most thrilling events in the Olympic Winter Games. Athletes spend years in training for their opportunity to race against the world's best—and against the clock. Just as in popular Summer Olympic sports such as track and swimming, speed skating features races that are decided by fractions of a second or by photo finishes.

Long Track and Short Track

Olympic speed skating is divided into two disciplines: *long track*, skated on a 400-meter oval; and *short track*, with a 111-meter track marked out on a hockey rink. Long-track racing has been in the Olympics since the very first Winter Games in 1924. Because of its tremendous popularity with fans and its appeal to the important worldwide television audience, short-track competition was elevated from a demonstration sport at the 1988 Calgary Olympics to an official medal sport starting with the 1992 Albertville Games.

Long-track competition consists of five races each for men and women. Both compete at 500, 1,000, 1,500, and 5,000 meters. The women also have a 3,000-meter event, and the men race

10,000 meters (the equivalent of 6.2 miles, the same "10K" familiar to recreational joggers).

At the Olympic level, the short-track races are the 500, 1,000 and 1,500 meters. The short-track Olympic program also includes two four-person relay events (3,000 meters for women, 5,000 meters for men).

Both styles of Olympic speed skating offer great suspense. In long-track competition, skaters in most events get only one opportunity to race. They compete two at a time, one each on the inner and outer lanes of the oval. Their real competition, however, is the clock. Sometimes the luck of the draw places the two favorites in the same *pair*, so they race head-to-head. Of course, in events with more than two gold-medal contenders, skaters must take their turn and then wait to see how their times

Cy White / PHOTO ACTION USA

Eric Heiden looks on with approval (upper right)
as Bonnie Blair races toward a record-setting
time at the North American Split Second Showdown.

compare with those who compete later in the session. Sometimes the medals are up for grabs until the final pair.

The clock plays a less crucial role in short track, where head-to-head competition is all-important. Short-track races consist of a series of qualification races similar to the preliminary rounds of a track meet. There are between four and six skaters in each heat, and the rink gets very crowded. It's not unusual for a couple of athletes to get their skates tangled and fall. Officials had to restart one race at the 1991 World Championships six times because of falls in the first turn! When someone falls later in the race, the competition simply goes on, and the skater nearly always gets back up and rejoins the race. In short track, the championship race gives the best skaters the chance to race directly against one another. The skater whose foot crosses the finish line first is the winner. Often the skaters are so tightly packed that a finish-line camera must sort out the results. Short-track races are timed only so that lists of records can be kept.

Origins of the Sport

For almost as long as people have populated northern climates, they have used some form of ice skates for transportation. Some historians believe skating began as an extension of skiing or snowshoeing, with polished animal bones or pieces of highly waxed wood serving as the runners. Scandinavian literature includes numerous references to skating on an iron skate as early as the year 200.

Over the centuries, refinements were made in equipment, and ice skating became a recreational activity in the 1300s. One breakthrough was the creation in Scotland in 1572 of a pair of all-iron skates. It should come as no surprise, then, that the first known ice skating club in the world was the Skating Club of Edinburgh. The first recorded speed skating competition took place in England in 1763, after which clubs and racing spread quickly throughout Europe. Laborers whose daily work gave them practice in skating fast over frozen canals were the primary competitors; the aristocrats gravitated toward artistic skating.

As skating spread to the United States, American inventors began to experiment with new materials for skates. E. W. Bushnell of Philadelphia is credited with making the first all-steel skate, in 1850. Steel blades were far lighter in weight than iron ones, and stayed sharp for months. The new blades led to the organization of speed skating as an international sport. The first World Championships were held in 1889 in the Netherlands, bringing together the Dutch, Russian, American, and English champions. The introduction of steel blades also gave birth to competitive figure skating. Fittingly, the *International Skating Union*, formed in 1892, still governs both speed skating and figure skating today.

Early Olympic Events

Speed skating has been included in the Olympics since the first Winter Games in 1924, generally with skaters competing just two at a time against the stopwatch. Those inaugural Winter Games featured four distances for men: 500, 1,500, 5,000, and 10,000 meters. Early on, skaters competed at Mother Nature's whim. Until artificially refrigerated skating ovals became available, competition took place on frozen lakes. On racing days, ice conditions got better or worse as the air temperature fell or rose, and performances varied accordingly.

The 1932 Games at Lake Placid, New York, were notable for the unusual circumstances under which the speed skating competition took place. With the approval of international officials, organizers called for the races to be conducted under North American rules, with athletes skating in a pack instead of two at a time in prescribed lanes. European skaters were outraged—some even boycotted the races, leaving just six countries in the competition. Not surprisingly, 10 of the 12 medalists were from the United States or Canada.

By the 1948 Games, advances in aviation brought new opportunities for American skaters. No longer did Olympic teams have to be chosen a full year in advance to permit athletes to travel by steamship to the Games in Europe, although the practice of picking teams with a year's lead time actually continued until the mid-1950s. Occasionally, U.S. skaters went abroad for World Championship competition.

Improvements in timing devices have allowed speed skating medal winners to be determined with increased precision. Until the late 1960s, races were timed only to the 10th of a second. At the 1968 Games in Grenoble, France, for instance, three American women were credited with the same time in the 500 meters, and all were awarded silver medals. Four years later, at Sapporo, Japan, officials began timing skaters to the 100th of a second, and there have been no ties since.

The Growth Years

Speed skating entered a new era at the 1960 Games in Squaw Valley, California, with the addition of women's events to the Olympic schedule. The Olympic Charter requiring that newly added sports must be practiced in at least 25 countries was conveniently ignored—23 women from just 10 nations entered. Women from the United States, Canada, and elsewhere had raced in three distances in 1932, but those events, along with competition in curling and dog-sled racing, were considered unofficial.

Another innovation at the 1960 Games was the construction of the world's first artificially refrigerated 400-meter oval. It measured 561 feet long by 231 feet wide, with the track itself a spacious 66 feet wide. Organizers even had snow-removal equipment standing by in case the ice needed to be cleared. Still, some teams were skeptical of the ice quality during the training sessions. Their concerns were set aside when one men's world record was broken and another was tied; all the women's races, of course, were new Olympic records.

In 1964, with the Soviet Union emerging as a world skating power, the United States captured just one Olympic gold medal in speed skating. Concerned politicians and speed skating boosters pushed for the construction of a refrigerated skating oval to ensure the development of American talent. The result was the Wisconsin Olympic Ice Rink in Milwaukee, which opened in 1966 and served as the nation's primary training and competition venue for the next 26 years.

Refrigeration equipment was installed at the 400-meter oval in Lake Placid for the 1980 Olympics, and the Americans received another priceless boost in the form of Eric Heiden's unprecedented five gold medals. The last Olympics of that decade, the 1988 Calgary Games, marked the introduction of short-track competition, greatly expanding Olympic opportunities for speed skaters.

Indoor Long Track Skating Ovals

Although better equipment and enhanced training techniques led to steady improvements in long-track world records through the mid-1980s, an exciting new chapter in the sport was written toward the end of the decade. In the Netherlands in 1987, for the first time, a 400-meter speed skating oval was equipped with a roof, providing better ice for workouts and racing. Skaters, spectators, and officials all quickly became accustomed to climate-controlled conditions. In addition, enclosed rinks made it possible to conduct events in the evening and without weather delays—no trivial matter for television networks seeking large prime-time audiences. The 1988 Calgary Olympics, the first conducted in an enclosed rink, produced world records in seven of the 10 events on the schedule.

Olympic races returned to an outdoor rink for the 1992 Games in Albertville, France. The weather was often dreary. Rain and soft ice affected several events, and not a single world or Olympic record was broken. Speed skating returned to an enclosed rink

Cy White / PHOTO ACTION USA

Pettit National Ice Center, Milwaukee, Wisconsin

for the 1994 Games—the spectacular "Viking Ship" in Hamar, Norway—and two world and five Olympic records fell.

In 1998 at Nagano, Japan, excellent conditions at the "M-Wave," along with the introduction of *clap skates* (more on those in Chapter 6), contributed to world records in five events and Olympic records in the other five. Nagano also saw the introduction of a second race in the 500 meters, with the times of the two runs combined to determine the standings. This came about because indoor ice is so fast that 500-meter skaters find it difficult to maintain their control when skating the final turn on the inner lane. With two runs, each skater gets to race once on each lane.

Clearly, indoor ovals are the way of the future. Some coaches believe World Championships should be staged only at enclosed ovals. An indoor facility at Kearns, Utah, opened in advance of the 2002 Olympics, and an enclosed facility is planned for the 2006 Olympics in Turin, Italy. Although host cities are not yet required to stage Olympic speed skating races in an enclosed rink, surely such facilities will be considered essential for a successful Games.

U.S. Medalists and Facilities

The opening of refrigerated ovals in Butte, Montana, in 1987 and in Roseville, Minnesota, in 1993 made an important contribution to speed skating in the United States. In 1992 the Milwaukee outdoor oval was replaced by the Pettit National Ice Center, which until 2001 was the nation's only enclosed 400-meter rink. The Pettit Center is credited with helping to prolong the careers of Dan Jansen and Bonnie Blair until the 1994 Olympics, at which both won gold medals.

Those victories extended American speed skating's remarkable record of accomplishment. Including Chris Witty's two medals in Nagano in 1998, U.S. speed skaters have won 54 Olympic medals—more than in any other winter sport and better than one-third of the U.S. all-time Winter Olympics total.

Cy White / PHOTO ACTION USA

Chris Witty with her silver and bronze medals from Nagano

Yet another assault on the record books came in March 2001, when the $29-million Utah Olympic Oval opened in Kearns. This facility combines the advantages of indoor ice with altitude (4,700 feet above sea level), giving skaters their fastest rink ever. In its three-day debut meet, the Utah Olympic Oval witnessed five world records and 57 national records.

With more and better 400-meter ovals serving long-track skaters and new hockey rinks providing expanded opportunities for short-track hopefuls, U.S. speed skating is poised for continued success.

Salt Lake City, 2002

Speed skating enjoyed a high profile in the planning for the 2002 Games. The schedule makers put speed skating events on nearly every day of the Olympic competition. Long-track events were scheduled for the Utah Olympic Oval, already renowned for its terrific skating conditions. (Although the oval is actually located in suburban Kearns, for the sake of simplicity we'll refer to the 2002 events as taking place in Salt Lake City.) When the figure skaters got days off from executing their triple jumps and dizzying spins at the Salt Lake Ice Center downtown, the short-trackers were assigned to race there.

In general, while the Olympics are more pressure-packed than other meets, the competition schedule is easier. During the World Cup or World Championships, a long-track skater will race up to twice a day, two days in a row. The Olympic schedule, however, allows for at least a day off between events. The lone exception is the 500-meter competition, which is designed as a back-to-back series of two heats. Results in the 500 are based on combining the times of the two runs.

The short-track athletes face a bit more challenging schedule, with individual and relay races in the same session. For skaters who compete in both, the Olympics are a test of pace, concentration, and stamina.

2002 Olympic Long Track Schedule

Saturday, February 9:	Men's 5,000 meters
Sunday, February 10:	Ladies' 3,000 meters
Monday, February 11:	Men's 500-meter preliminary
Tuesday, February 12:	Men's 500-meter final
Wednesday, February 13:	Ladies' 500-meter preliminary
Thursday, February 14:	Ladies' 500-meter final
Saturday, February 16:	Men's 1,000 meters
Sunday, February 17:	Ladies' 1,000 meters
Tuesday, February 19:	Men's 1,500 meters
Wednesday, February 20:	Ladies' 1,500 meters
Friday, February 22:	Men's 10,000 meters
Saturday, February 23:	Ladies' 5,000 meters

2002 Olympic Short Track Schedule

Wednesday, February 13:

Ladies' 1,500 meters

Men's 1,000-meter preliminary

Men's 5,000-meter relay preliminary

Saturday, February 16:

Ladies' 500-meter preliminary and final

Ladies' 3,000-meter relay preliminary

Men's 1,000-meter final

Wednesday, February 20:

Ladies' 3,000-meter relay final

Ladies' 1,000-meter preliminary

Men's 1,500-meter final

Saturday, February 23:

Ladies' 1,000-meter final

Men's 500-meter preliminary and final

Men's 5,000-meter relay final

2

Stars of Today

LONG TRACK

KC Boutiette (USA)

Whether on wheels or steel blades, when KC Boutiette laces up his skates, get ready for excitement. KC is a versatile athlete who can be competitive at all five Olympic speed skating distances, can race marathons on ice, and has been a world champion inliner at 100 kilometers.

KC was born on April 11, 1970, in Tacoma, Washington; by the way, the KC doesn't stand for anything. He shocked the speed skating establishment by winning the 5,000 and 10,000 meters at the 1994 U.S. Olympic Trials. At that time, he was hardly known outside the world of inline racing and had been on ice skates for just two months. While he was unable to achieve the necessary qualifying times for the long races in Lillehammer, Norway, he did get his first Olympic experience that year by competing in the 1,500 meters, placing 39th.

The four years between Lillehammer and Nagano helped KC refine his ice-skating form and get adjusted to clap skates. In 1998 he began the Games with a 14th place in the 5,000 meters, then recorded three top-10 finishes (fifth in the 1,500, eighth in the 1,000, and eighth in the 10,000). In the 2001 World Allround Championships, he placed 15th overall; in the World Single Distance Championships, his best showing was eighth in the 5,000. "When he does something special," says Dutch great Gianni Romme, "he can be dangerous."

In the end, KC's greatest contribution to speed skating may be the encouragement he gave to other inliners who wanted to try the ice. Three other former inliners joined KC on the '98 Olympic team, and there could be as many as seven ex-inliners (including one short-track specialist) racing in 2002.

Cy White / PHOTO ACTION USA

Casey FitzRandolph (USA)

Born on January 21, 1975, Casey FitzRandolph was just five years old when he took to the ice with Eric Heiden's speed skating club in Madison, Wisconsin. Ever since, Casey has worked to become an Olympic gold medalist like his hero.

Casey was rising to the top of the U.S. sprint ranks at the same time Dan Jansen was ready to retire. Casey stepped in and won his first national title in 1994–95, when he also raced in his first World Sprints. He took another step up when he captured the overall bronze medal in the 1997 Worlds and set an American record in the 1,000 meters.

The Olympic season of 1997–98 proved frustrating for Casey, however. He had more difficulty than most skaters adjusting to the new clap skates and was unsure of himself heading to Nagano. But he rebounded just before the Games. Casey stood in third place after the first 500-meter race, then had a slower skate the second day to end up in sixth place. He shrugged off his disappointment and, five days later, placed seventh in the 1,000.

His equipment woes solved, Casey grabbed two World Cup medals in 1998–99. A few months later, he left the American coaches to move to Calgary and work out with Canada's record-setting sprint team. He won medals at two early World Cups in 1999–2000, then faced another setback—a broken sternum suffered in a car accident that kept him out of the U.S. National Championships.

Determined to reestablish himself as a contender in 2000–01, Casey fought off younger challengers and grabbed back his American title. He won three medals in World Cup races and capped his season by winning the bronze in the 500 meters at the World Single Distance Championships.

Cy White / PHOTO ACTION USA

Catriona Le May Doan (Canada)

Like Bonnie Blair, who was 30 when she won her final World Sprints title, Catriona Le May Doan is only going faster as her career approaches its end. In the 2000–01 season, at the age of 30, Catriona was dominant in the 500 meters, winning nine of 10 World Cups and setting the world record (plus the world record under the *samalog* point system) at the Canadian championships. Then she hit the ice at the Utah Olympic Oval and recorded 500-meter times of 37.43 seconds and a world record 37.29, not only winning the World Single Distance Championship but also erasing the previous world record in the combined 500 meters. Catriona proved strong in the 1,000 as well, capturing the bronze medal at the World Single Distance meet. "I never broke under pressure during the entire season," she said. "I'm where I want to be heading into the Olympic year."

Born December 23, 1970, and a skater since the age of 10, Catriona steadily climbed the world rankings during the early 1990s. Then she made a huge jump at the right time, going from fifth at the 1997 World Sprints to the medals podium at the 1998 Nagano Games. Catriona won the first run of the Olympic 500 meters in a meet-record time; she also had a strong second run to capture the gold and lead a 1-2 Canada sweep. Later in the Games, Catriona claimed the bronze medal in the 1,000.

Cy White / PHOTO ACTION USA

Gunda (Kleemann) Niemann-Stirnemann (Germany)

With eight Olympic medals and a record nine World Allround titles going into Salt Lake City, Gunda (Kleemann) Niemann-Stirnemann is one of speed skating's true superstars. Gunda had the good fortune to begin her international career just as the 5,000 meters, one of her best distances, was added to the Olympic schedule. But Gunda has also had her share of bad luck.

Gunda, who was born September 7, 1966, in Sondershausen, Germany, was a national-caliber 400-meter hurdler before she became a speed skater with the Erfurt Sport Club, a rival of the powerful Dresden club. At age 21 she earned a spot on the East German Olympic speed skating team for the 1988 Calgary Olympics. There, she posted seventh-place finishes in the 1,500 and 5,000 meters. Four years later, Gunda raced to gold medals in the 3,000 and 5,000. She was favored to win the 1,500, too. But she couldn't match the time of her teammate Jacqueline Börner, whose victory completed a fairy-tale comeback from injuries in a hit-and-run car accident, and settled for the silver medal.

Misfortune of another type disrupted Gunda's game plan at the 1994 Olympics. Racing around the oval at the Viking Ship early in the 3,000-meter race, Gunda inadvertently stepped on a lane marker and fell. That stumble stunned the crowd because Gunda had not lost a 3,000 in three years. A few days later, she did pick up a bronze medal in the 1,500. She had a last chance at victory in the 5,000, where she was the defending Olympic champion. Gunda was ahead of the leader's pace until the final lap, but couldn't hold on. Although Gunda did win the silver medal, the world's top-ranked female middle- and long-distance skater ended up in 1994 without a single Olympic gold.

Years of demanding training and top-level racing take their toll on an athlete, and in December 1995, Gunda needed arthroscopic surgery on her right knee. Only two months later she was able to repeat as World Allround champion.

The third knee surgery of her career came the summer before the Nagano Olympics. Still, Gunda medaled in all three of her Olympic events in 1998. She won gold in the 3,000 meters and silvers in the 1,500 and 5,000, losing only to world-record performances. Including Nagano, Gunda's Olympic medal haul stood at eight, matching the total of her early rival Karin Kania (see Chapter 10).

Remarkably, at age 34, Gunda captured the 3,000- and 5,000-meter titles at the 2001 World Single Distance Championships; the 5,000 was a world record by nearly three seconds. No wonder some call her Gunda the Great.

Cy White / PHOTO ACTION USA

Derek Parra (USA)

While it's true that Derek Parra retired from inline skating in 1996, one thing he is not is a quitter. Derek, born on March 15, 1970, showed his toughness at the 1995 Pan American Games in Argentina. When he was about halfway through skating the inline marathon race, a pace car pulled out and struck him. Derek peeled himself off the pavement and rejoined the leaders, then used his power on the late uphill stages of the course and pulled away to win the gold by about two minutes. It was his eighth medal of the meet (five golds, two silvers, and one bronze), making him the most-decorated athlete in any sport at the 1995 Games.

Derek grew up in San Bernardino, California, and started on roller skates when he was 14. During a long career on wheels, he won 18 World Championship gold medals, including three golds at the 1993 world inline meet. He first tried ice speed skating in December 1995 at age 24. He was a quick study, qualifying for his first World Cup just a few months later.

In 1998 he earned a spot on the U.S. Olympic team in the 5,000 meters and traveled to Nagano. However, his best time coming into the Games did not rank him among the world's 32 fastest, so he didn't get to skate. Disappointed, Derek set out to gain important experience the next two seasons in World Cup competition, the World Allround Championships, and the World Single Distance Championships. Derek entered the 2002 Olympic season on a high after his best placement ever at the World Allround Championships (13th overall) and a silver medal in the 1,500 meters at the 2001 World Single Distance Championships in Salt Lake City.

Cy White / PHOTO ACTION USA

Claudia Pechstein (Germany)

If her career hadn't coincided with that of the spectacular Gunda Niemann-Stirnemann, Claudia Pechstein might well be called speed skating's distance queen. Then again, without Niemann-Stirnemann to push her, Pechstein might never have reached the lofty heights she has.

Claudia has won five Olympic medals, including two golds, and captured the 2000 World Allround Championship after four runner-up finishes to Gunda. Claudia collected a bronze medal (behind Niemann's gold) in the 5,000 meters at her first Olympics, in 1992. Two years later, at Lillehammer, Claudia captured another bronze, this time in the 3,000. Claudia's performance was even more outstanding in the 5,000, as she skated a personal-best time by a stunning 19.21 seconds to claim her first Olympic gold medal. Nagano brought Claudia a silver medal in the 3,000 (behind Gunda's Olympic-record skate) and a gold in the 5,000, a world-record performance that was just four-hundredths of a second ahead of Gunda.

Another German, Anni Friesinger, was crowned the 2001 World Allround champion just ahead of Claudia. At the World Single Distance Championships, Claudia collected a silver medal in the 5,000 meters (behind Gunda) and a bronze in the 3,000 (trailing only Gunda and Anni).

Born on February 22, 1971, and on skates since the age of three, Claudia has had an impressive career and been a key part of Germany's domination of women's distance skating.

Rintje Ritsma and Gianni Romme (Netherlands)

Keep an eye on this duo, if you can. Rintje and Gianni are so equally talented that they often end up skating in the same pair. Look closely and you can tell them apart. Rintje is about a half-inch shorter and nearly 20 pounds heavier.

Gianni (born February 12, 1973) grabbed the spotlight away from Rintje with his world-record, gold-medal race in the 5,000 in Nagano. He dipped more than 15 seconds under the existing Olympic record when he won the 10,000. Still, it took until 2000 for Gianni to win his first World Allround title. He left nothing to chance in the final race of that meet—he lapped the skater with whom he was paired, eventual runner-up Ids Postma.

The victory completed a circuitous rise to the top for Gianni, who had started skating at the late age of 13 and made his first national team only when Dutch native Bart Veldkamp began to compete for Belgium in 1995. "I have no limits," Gianni once said. Incidentally, Gianni is coached by Peter Mueller, who coached Bonnie Blair and Dan Jansen to Olympic victories in 1992 and '94.

In 2001, Rintje reclaimed the world title without winning any of the four events. Previously, Rintje had been world champion in 1995, '96, and '99. He also is a six-time European champion. Rintje (born April 13, 1970) began his Olympic career with a fourth-place performance in the 1,500-meter race at the 1992 Games. Two years later, he captured the silver in that race behind Norwegian hero Johann Olav Koss and a bronze in the 5,000 (plus a seventh-place showing in the 10,000). Nagano brought Rintje medals in all three of his Olympic races—silver in the 5,000 (behind Gianni), bronze in the 1,500, and a bronze in the 10,000 that completed a 1-2-3 sweep by the Netherlands.

As the 2002 Olympics approached, both skaters had something to prove after how their seasons went in 2000–01. Gianni declined the chance to defend his gold medal at the World

Allround Championships because of a lingering illness. At the World Single Distance Championships, he managed just a bronze in the 5,000. Rintje, meanwhile, won the world title, but skated only one event at the World Single Distance meet (the 1,500) and finished back in 13th place.

Jennifer Rodriguez (USA)

Jennifer Rodriguez could do some pretty fancy stuff on roller skates, but she knew it would never get her to the Olympic Games. So after winning World Championships and, in 1995, a Pan American Games bronze medal, she took the advice of KC Boutiette and made the move to the ice in 1996. By qualifying for four events at the 1998 Games, Jennifer (born June 8, 1976) became the first American of Hispanic descent on a Winter Olympic team.

Jennifer made her Olympic debut one to remember. In the first women's event on the schedule, the 3,000 meters, Jennifer dipped under the Olympic record and finished with a stunning fourth-place showing. As the Games moved along, Jennifer finished in eighth place in the 1,500, 13th place in the 1,000, and, finally, 10th place in the 5,000. American speed skating had a new star.

After Nagano, Jennifer returned to a limited schedule of inline races yet continued her strong performances on the ice. Twice she won 500-meter silver medals at the World Allround Championships, and in seven races at the World Single Distance Championships she placed no worse than 10th. She even broke Chris Witty's American record in the 1,500 meters. "Ice is my love now," she says.

Jennifer and KC got engaged in 1999 and soon after moved to Salt Lake City to prepare for the Olympics. She has the range to be competitive in all five Olympic distances. Regardless of the results, Jennifer knows she has followed her heart. "I've won the Worlds on inlines," she once said, "but going to the Olympics is everyone's dream."

Cy White / PHOTO ACTION USA

Hiroyasu Shimizu (Japan)

Competing in the Olympics in your home country is the dream of every athlete, and Hiroyasu Shimizu made the most of his opportunity in 1998. Due to a change in the Olympic schedule, Hiroyasu had to skate two 500-meter races on successive days to win a gold medal. But he didn't collapse under the pressure. He skated an Olympic record to grab the lead after the first day; then, with Crown Prince Naruhito and Princess Masako in attendance, Hiroyasu broke that record to win the gold by nearly a half-second. A few days later, Hiroyasu collected a bronze in the 1,000.

Hiroyasu (born February 27, 1974) recorded a fifth-place finish in the 500 at the 1994 Olympics and was given a spot on the team for Nagano a full two and one-half years before the opening ceremony. Like Casey FitzRandolph, Hiroyasu had great trouble adjusting to the clap skates that came on the scene in 1996. He was the last man on his team to make the switch, just three months before the '98 Games.

Hiroyasu etched his name in the record books again in 2000–01 when he skated a world record 34.32 seconds in the 500 meters at the World Single Distance Championships. His time was a remarkable improvement over Nagano, where the two runs that combined to give him the '98 Olympic gold were 35.76 and 35.59. Hiroyasu's other run at the World Single Distance meet was 34.64, giving him a world record for the combined times. Hiroyasu finished as overall runner-up to Canada's Michael Ireland at the 2001 World Sprint Championships. In fact, Hiroyasu has yet to win a World Sprints overall championship— he's been the silver medalist four times, including in 2001.

Bart Veldkamp (Belgium)

Speed skating is one of the most popular spectator sports in the Netherlands. Olympic victories prompt national celebrations. And when an athlete performs at less than his or her expected level, the questions and criticism come quickly.

Bart Veldkamp is an exceptional skater who proved he could thrive both in the intense environment of the Dutch program and outside it. Bart, born on November 22, 1967, rose through the ranks in the late 1980s and early '90s to earn a trip to his first Olympics, the 1992 Games in Albertville. He started out with a fifth-place showing in the 5,000, then won the 10,000 to give the Netherlands its first men's gold medal in speed skating since 1976. Bart celebrated his win by spraying champagne around the room at his post-race press conference.

At Lillehammer in 1994 the great Johann Olav Koss, buoyed by waves of cheers from his Norwegian fans, won both the 5,000 and 10,000. Veldkamp managed a bronze medal in the 10,000 and (as at Albertville) a fifth-place finish in the 5,000.

The 10,000 is Bart's favorite event, but it is rarely contested on the World Cup circuit. To qualify to skate it at the European or World Allround Championships, Bart would normally have had to beat out fierce competition from within the Dutch team. Rather than face that challenge, Bart pursued an alternative strategy. In 1995 he left the Dutch team and sought to race for Belgium.

Just seven months before the Nagano Games, Bart was granted Belgian citizenship. He was the only speed skater at the 1998 Olympics to represent Belgium, which had won just four medals in Winter Olympic history, most recently in 1948. "I was born in Holland, I changed to Belgium," Veldkamp said at Nagano. "But if you start looking at the moon and ask where I come from, I will tell you the earth."

Bart went for broke in his pair in the 5,000 meters, establishing a world record some two seconds faster than the previous mark. However, two Dutch skaters who competed after Bart did even better, bumping him down to the bronze medal. Any animosity Bart may have felt toward the Dutch team was forgotten on the awards stand as he and the other medalists playfully posed for photographers. Later in the Games, Bart finished just 1.5 seconds out of the bronze-medal position in the 10,000. Bart narrowly missed winning the 2001 European Championship and placed a strong third overall at the 2001 World Allround Championships.

Chris Witty (USA)

At age nine, Chris Witty won her first speed skating race so handily she already was showing off her medal before the second-place finisher crossed the line. But that doesn't mean that everything has always come easy for America's sprint star. Chris nearly had to give up skating when she was about 12 years old because her father had lost his job and money was tight. The family persevered, and Chris, the youngest of four kids, continued to improve—all the way to two Olympic medals in 1998.

Chris began her Olympic career at the 1994 Lillehammer Games, earning the No. 2 spot on the U.S. team in the 1,000 meters behind Bonnie Blair. Chris finished 23rd in the Olympics, and with Bonnie's retirement in 1995, many began calling Chris "the next Bonnie Blair." Chris may have been a little uncomfortable with that title, but she proved worthy of it in 1996 when she succeeded Bonnie as the World Sprints champion. Later in '96, Chris earned the alternate's berth on the cycling team for the Atlanta Summer Games.

With the calendar edging closer to the Nagano Olympics, Chris began to show the consistently high results that made other skaters take notice. She won nine World Cup medals and the overall bronze at the World Sprints in 1996–97. In just the second meet of the 1997–98 season, Chris showed she was ready to go for the gold, setting a world record in the 1,000 meters. From then until Nagano, Chris lost only once in the 1,000.

Cy White / PHOTO ACTION USA

Few athletes at Nagano were as heavily favored as Chris was in the 1,000. She was in the best shape of her life, and the Olympic schedule was on her side—her best event would come late in the Games. Clearly, she had come a long way since paying for equipment with the paper-route money she earned in her hometown of West Allis, Wisconsin. Chris started the Olympics by finishing 10th in the 500 meters, and her confidence grew with a bronze medal in the 1,500 meters. But in the 1,000, Chris lacked something. She couldn't match the pace of Dutch star Marianne Timmer, who skated just before her. Marianne walked off with her second gold medal of the Games, with Chris taking the silver about three-tenths of a second behind. Chris quickly shook off her disappointment and finished the season strong. In the final meet of the year, Chris skated a world record of 1 minute, 14.96 seconds—the first woman ever to skate the 1,000 in less than 1:15.

While turning in excellent results on the ice from 1998 to spring 2000, Chris also devoted herself to cycling training for the 2000 Summer Games. She became only the ninth American ever to compete in both the Winter and Summer Olympics when she raced the 500-meter time trial in Sydney. She placed fifth, one of the best finishes by any U.S. cyclist.

Chris, who was born June 23, 1975, was inconsistent during the 2000–01 season. She placed seventh in the World Sprints but later broke a world record in the 1,000 meters that had stood for two years. In her final meet of the season, she twice broke her own American record in the 500 meters.

Chris is so well respected that some up-and-coming sprinters are called "the next Chris Witty." It seems Chris can handle almost anything that comes her way. "I've told young skaters it's good to respect and look up to their competitors," she says. "But you have to go to the starting line and realize your own potential and say, 'Why not?' "

Jeremy Wotherspoon (Canada)

Heading into the 2002 Olympics, tall (6' 2") and powerful Jeremy Wotherspoon was already a two-time World Sprints champion and the winner of four consecutive World Cup overall titles in the 1,000 meters. When he raced at the Utah Olympic Oval at the 2001 World Single Distance Championships, he lost his 500-meter world record but took away the 1,000 mark from teammate Michael Ireland. "I like the ice here," Jeremy said. "I knew these kinds of times were possible."

Jeremy skated both short track and long track until 1994, when he moved from his home in Humboldt, Saskatchewan, to Calgary to train on the famed Olympic Oval there. Born on October 26, 1976, he was fresh out of high school at the time and just beginning to show his talent.

The 1997–98 season was his breakthrough year, with World Cup titles in both the 500 and 1,000, World Single Distance medals in both events, and the overall silver at the World Sprints. Then there was Nagano, where Jeremy rallied from seventh place after the first race in the 500 meters to lead Canada's 2-3-4-5 sweep of the final standings. His silver was the Canadian men's first long-track speed skating medal since 1984. Jeremy also placed sixth in the 1,000.

Jeremy is an avid outdoorsman and enjoys fishing with training partner Casey FitzRandolph of the United States.

SHORT TRACK

Apolo Anton Ohno (USA)

It's a good thing Apolo Anton Ohno added 30 pounds of muscle in the past four years. He needs it to haul around all the medals he's been winning.

This 5' 8", 165-pound dynamo had a great season in 2000–01. He won the 3,000 meters and the overall individual silver medal, and helped the American team to gold in the 5,000-meter relay at the World Championships. In World Cup racing, he was nearly unbeatable. Not only did Apolo claim wins in season-long rankings in the 500, 1,000, and 1,500, but he also picked up the overall title in the series. Earlier in the season, he scored his third U.S. Championship. That's a lot of hardware for an 18-year-old!

Apolo started out on roller skates at about age seven and raced on quad-style skates before switching to inline competition. After watching the 1994 Olympics on television, he decided to give the ice a try and, like many inliners, was a quick study. His talent was so evident that officials bent the minimum-age rules and admitted him to the program at the U.S. Olympic Training Center in Lake Placid, New York, when Apolo was just 14 years old. Within months, he placed third at the U.S. Junior Championships. Then, in March 1997, Apolo raced to the top of the podium at the U.S. Senior Championships.

The 1997–98 season, including the Olympic Trials, proved to be a challenge for Apolo. In the six-race meet, he managed just a fifth-place finish in one 500-meter time trial and wound up 16th overall. The slump was mercifully short-lived, with Apolo winning the National Championship and the World Junior overall gold medal the following season.

Apolo was born on May 22, 1982, and grew up in Seattle. His dad, Yuki, created his name by combining the Greek words *apo*, meaning "away," and *lo*, meaning "look out."

"I like pack-style for the excitement," Apolo once said. With bright young stars like Apolo, no wonder fans are excited about short-track skating.

Amy Peterson (USA)

She's been a participant in every Olympic short-track competition, even when the races were designated only as demonstration events. Yet relatively few people know of Amy Peterson.

Amy's Olympic performances have been overshadowed by those of teammate Cathy Turner, whose Olympic career included two gold medals, a silver, and a bronze. Amy is right behind in total medals, with one silver and two bronzes. Moreover, she was the only U.S. woman to reach the finals at the 1998 Games, finishing fourth in the 1,000 meters.

Amy has won an impressive eight national titles, including the National Championship in 2000–01. She helped the U.S. finish fifth in the 3,000-meter relay at the 2001 World Championships. On the World Cup circuit, she captured one bronze medal in the 500 meters and another bronze in the relay. Overall, Amy finished the season No. 9 in the World Cup rankings.

Amy was born on November 29, 1971. Her mother and two of her sisters also were speed skaters; her uncle, Gene Sandvig, was a three-time Olympic speed skater. No wonder two-year-old Amy took to the ice! She skated on the many rinks and lakes near her home in Maplewood, Minnesota, and even competed in figure skating until she was 14.

Amy's first Olympics came in 1988, when short track was a demonstration sport and the U.S. placed fifth in the 3,000-meter relay. Amy raced in all four individual events on that year's schedule, but didn't advance out of the opening heats in any of them. The race experience proved valuable, though, as Amy established herself as the U.S. team's most consistent performer over the next few years.

Short track gained official Olympic status in 1992, when Amy helped the Americans win the silver medal in the 3,000-meter relay. Two years later, it was a relay bronze and a 500-meter bronze (behind Cathy Turner) for Amy.

Amy's rankings slipped after the Lillehammer Games because of mononucleosis and chronic fatigue syndrome, yet she rallied to win the 1998 U.S. Olympic Trials. At Nagano she placed fourth in the 1,000 meters and helped her team to fifth in the 3,000-meter relay. Since then, she's won three straight National Championships.

Yang Yang (A) and Yang Yang (S) (China)

This talented duo can make fans feel like they're seeing double. But despite their similar names, these two women aren't even related. In fact, in Chinese their names are written differently and mean different things. Yang Yang (A) means "flying flag," and Yang Yang (S) means "sunshine." The initials are meaningless in Chinese; they're used to help Westerners tell these athletes apart.

Both women were born in northeastern China, Yang Yang (A) on August 24, 1976, in Heilongjiang Province, and Yang Yang (S) on September 14, 1977, in Jilin.

Yang Yang (S) got her first Olympic experience in 1994, before she had even skated in her first World Championships. At the Lillehammer Games, Yang Yang (S) placed fifth in the 1,000 meters and eighth in the 500. It appeared that she would get a medal in the relay when the Chinese team crossed the finish line second. Some 20 minutes later, though, China was disqualified for having failed to get out of the way of the U.S. team after an exchange.

In Nagano, Yang Yang (S) and Yang Yang (A) put their names in the record books together by racing on China's silver-medal team in the 3,000-meter relay. Next came the individual events, and

Yang Yang (S) benefited when others suffered misfortune. In the 500-meter final, she had an early stumble and was out of the running until two other skaters tangled with one lap remaining. That allowed Yang Yang (S) to pick up the silver medal. Just after the 1,000, Yang Yang (A) was disqualified for interfering with another finalist near the finish line, and Yang Yang (S) was moved up to the second-place spot. That sent Yang Yang (A), the reigning world champion, home without an individual Olympic medal.

Since 1998, though, Yang Yang (A) has been the superior performer. She has won the past five overall gold medals at the World Championships, including victories in three of the four individual races at the 2001 meet. Yang Yang (S) placed fourth overall, and the two were part of the gold-medal relay.

For Further Information

Complete biographies of American skaters are available on US Speedskating's web site:

> http://www.usspeedskating.org/

For information on international performers, try these sites:

> http://www.saltlake2002.com/bios/index.html
>
> http://www.NBCOlympics.com/
>
> http://isu.cyberscoreboard.com/biography.php

3

Speed Skating Competitions

While speed skating draws most of its attention during the Olympics, world-caliber athletes compete extensively every year. And so do speed skaters at all levels.

The racing season runs from late October through early April for indoor competition. Outdoor races can be held from November to February, if weather permits.

Grassroots Competition

Let's talk first about competition for grassroots skaters. This means both the six-year-olds who dream of someday being Olympians and the adults who simply enjoy the fitness and social benefits of skating.

Remember that there are two types of speed skating: long track, skated on a 400-meter oval, and short track, on a 111-meter track. The most common type of meet is the short-track competition, which is held on a standard hockey rink. The United States has hundreds of hockey rinks, but just five 400-meter ovals.

Cy White / PHOTO ACTION USA

Shani Davis practices long-track speed skating.

A short-track meet usually includes races at four or five distances, appropriate to the age of the contestants. For instance, an 11-year-old could enter four races ranging from 333 meters (three laps) to 777 meters (seven laps). The races for 17-year-olds would go from 500 meters to 3,000 meters. There can be relay races, too.

Grassroots skaters can also participate in long-track meets. Distances range from 300 to 3,000 meters. What makes these races different from the Olympic-style events held at the same facilities is that the non-elite meets are contested *pack-style—*

that is, in groups of four to seven racers. In pack-style races, skaters don't have to stay in an assigned lane.

Whether in short- or long-track competition, the group of skaters is divided so that qualifying races can be run at each distance. Depending on the number of entries, a skater might have to compete in heats, quarterfinals, and semifinals before the final.

If you're competing at the grassroots level, you'll be spending the entire day at the rink, so come prepared! Bring all the skating gear and clothing you might need, some reading material and your personal CD player to kill time between races, and your favorite healthy snacks and sports drinks. Family members and other fans will find many of those items useful too, as well as a stadium blanket to use in the bleachers.

Elite Competition

Elite-level meets involve only a couple of hundred skaters nationwide. Many of these amazing athletes have been on skates since they were five years old, but there are exceptions, such as the competitors who came into the sport from inline skating.

Each year, there are national and international competitions for both long-track and short-track skaters. Athletes generally qualify for the World Championships by their performances in the U.S. Championships, which follow the same basic schedule of races.

The long-track World Allround Championships consist of a two- or three-day meet bringing together men and women who test themselves at sprint, middle-distance, and long-distance events. For women, the races are the 500 and 3,000 meters on the first day; for the men it's the 500 and 5,000. Both the women and the men skate 1,500 to begin the second day. The meet concludes with the 5,000 for women and the 10,000 for men— events that are a true test of the skaters' ability and conditioning. The World Championships began in 1889 for the men and in 1936 for the women.

The long-track skaters who focus on the shorter races compete in the World Sprint Championships. Here, both women and men have the same schedule of events: 500 and 1,000 meters on two successive days. The World Sprints began in Milwaukee, Wisconsin, in 1970.

Cy White / PHOTO ACTION USA

Dan Jansen rounds a turn in the 500-meter race.

With several races spread over two days, how do you know who won? Long-track speed skating employs a scoring system that converts an athlete's time into points. As in golf, the lowest score wins. The basis for this score, known as the *samalog*, is the time in the 500 meters. Here are two examples from U.S. skaters in recent championships.

Jennifer Rodriguez's 8th Place at the 2001 World Allround

Event	Time	Time in seconds	Divisor	Points
500m	40.29	40.29	1	40.290
3,000m	4:28.37	268.37	6	44.728
1,500m	2:06.85	126.85	3	42.283
5,000m	7:41.81	461.81	10	46.181
Total				173.482

Casey FitzRandolph's Victory at the 2001 U.S. Sprints

Event	Time	Time in seconds	Divisor	Points
500m	36.11	36.11	1	36.11
1,000m	1:11.54	71.54	2	35.77
500m	36.00	36.00	1	36.00
1,000m	1:11.48	71.48	2	35.74
Total				143.62

For additional information on samalog scoring, see Chapter 11.

Cy White / PHOTO ACTION USA

Dick Jansen, brother of Dan Jansen, rounds the turn, trying to stay close to the lane markers to avoid skating additional distance.

Since 1996, there has been a third type of international long-track competition: the World Single Distance Championships. At this exciting season-ending meet, a limited field of skaters who have qualified based on their year-long results compete in winner-take-all, Olympic-style races.

Other major events throughout the season include the World Cup series. For the younger skaters, there are the World Junior Championships (for skaters 19 and younger) and usually several "country matches," for up to six nations. The World Juniors is an allround meet. In 2001 a team pursuit event, similar to a relay, was added.

World-class short-trackers have the National Championships, a World Cup series, and the World University Games on their calendar. Elite short-trackers also compete in the World Team Championships, which began in 1991, and the more important World Championships. Officially, the World Championships originated in 1981, although an unofficial event was held in Champaign, Illinois, in 1976.

At the World Team Championships, athletes get points for their finishes in the 500, 1,000, 1,500, women's 3,000 relay, and men's 5,000 relay; the countries with the most points win the medals. The World Championships consist of the 500, 1,000, 1,500, and 3,000 meters for both men and women, the women's 3,000-meter relay, and the men's 5,000-meter relay. Skaters acquire points for their performances in individual races, thus deciding the overall medals. The United States picked up gold medals from Apolo Anton Ohno in the 3,000 meters and from the men's 5,000-meter relay squad in 2001. Bonnie Blair (1986) remains the only American ever to win the overall gold medal.

Spectator Tips

In several ways, watching a speed skating competition is like watching a track meet. In short-track racing, the competitors advance through preliminary rounds to a final, and the first person to cross the finish line is the winner. The 400-meter oval used in long-track skating is the same size as the running track that circles a football field. Each trip around the track is called a *lap*, and you can watch the scoreboard for the skaters' times for each one.

Although the competition format is different in the two disciplines, both long- and short-track skaters can be spurred on by the enthusiasm of the fans. Except for when the gun is up and the athletes are waiting for a race to begin, you can make all the noise you want.

In Europe, where speed skating enjoys its greatest popularity, spectators like to arrive early to sing folk songs to the accompaniment of small brass bands. Fans use drums, cowbells, and other noisemakers to encourage their favorites. They wave flags and hang banners around the rink. Many of these practices have become common at top-level U.S. meets, too. Some Dutch and Norwegian followers of the sport are so faithful they plan yearly vacations to World Cup and World Championship events in North America. You can recognize these fans by their painted faces and joyful attitude. Most European fans speak excellent English, so don't hesitate to ask them about their country's skaters. If you have a lapel pin or other sports souvenir, you may be able to swap it with a foreign visitor and come away with a special remembrance of an international competition.

Watching a Short Track Meet

Short-track meets provide the fan with several chances to watch the top competitors. As the field is whittled down by preliminary heats, watch to see which skaters race consistently well and which ones are barely advancing with each race.

Tactics come into play in every round. Usually only the top two qualify from each preliminary race, so you'll see skaters who try to break away from the crowd. Of course, with two athletes

Cy White / PHOTO ACTION USA

World-class American men skaters compete in a short-track race:
(left to right) Jeff Benjamin, Matt Renner, Charles King, Pat Wentland.

advancing in the competition, it's not necessary to finish first. A skater may be racing only as hard as needed to qualify. Sometimes the pace dawdles until the final lap or two, when everyone makes a mad chase for the coveted qualifying positions.

In short-track racing, an athlete can pass another either on the inside or on the outside. Passes must be made cleanly and without body contact. Officials will disqualify a skater who impedes another's progress. To pass in a crowded pack of four skaters requires great racing instincts and split-second timing.

Relays are fascinating to watch because each team determines how many laps each skater will race before handing off to a teammate—usually one, one and one-half, or two laps per leg. There are no batons. An exchange is made when the new skater is pushed from behind by the skater completing a leg.

Races are timed for record purposes, but what really counts is the order of finish of the final race. You won't see skaters leaning at the finish line like sprinters in a track meet. In speed skating, the order of finish is determined by when the foot crosses the finish line. Sometimes a photograph is needed to sort out the results.

Your best vantage point for watching a short-track competition is in the bleachers, several rows up. Any closer and your view could be obscured by the dasher boards, by the protective glass, or by officials in the infield.

Watching a Long Track Meet

In long-track speed skating (also called *metric* skating), the clock is what counts. Skaters race in pairs, trying to beat the times of those who have competed in previous pairs and/or establish a time that later competitors will try to beat. Most times, a skater who falls doesn't bother to resume the race because too much time has already been lost to place among the contenders.

When you first arrive at a long-track meet, get a copy of the pairing sheet so you can follow the action. The pairing sheet

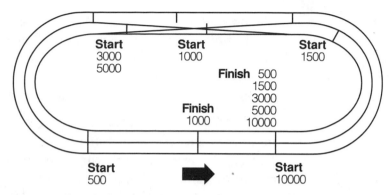

Diagram of a standard speed skating track illustrates staggered starts and the crossover pattern used in Olympic competition.

will identify the skaters in each pair with an "I" or an "O." This refers to the lane in which the skater begins the race—*inner* (I) or *outer* (O). The skaters switch lanes each lap to equalize the distance, but the skater who began on the inner lane is listed on the scoreboard throughout the race as the inner skater, and the skater who began on the outer lane is always listed as the outer skater. A pairing sheet may list the order of events and the world, national, and track records for each distance. At international competitions, the pairing sheet also lists each skater's country (see Chapter 11 for the commonly used national abbreviations).

Because of the physical demands of speed skating, athletes take care to pace themselves through long-distance races. Watch the scoreboard to see whether a long-distance racer is skating even *splits* or slowing down with each lap. It's very rare for a skater to get faster as the race progresses. A good public address announcer will tell the crowd if a skater is on pace for a record of some type, such as a *personal best* (often called simply a *personal*).

Most 400-meter ovals are equipped with sophisticated scoreboards that post the lap splits of each pair relative to the current leader in the competition. In the sprint events, the board will provide the times of the skaters' *openers*. The openers are the very first split times—for example, the first 100 meters of a

500-meter race—and tell you how good a skater is at getting off the starting line. Overall times and standings are flashed after each pair so you can see how all the competitors are doing. At many meets, officials make stacks of photocopies of the final results and pass them through the crowd—a great way to keep track of what you've just watched.

It's also fun to compare the skating styles of the different competitors. Does the skater glide a long time with each stroke, or have a quick turnover in the legs? Watch how explosive a skater is from the starting line, how close she stays to the lane markers in the turns, and how smoothly she switches lanes on the backstretch of each lap. If you see a long-distance skater unable to keep his arms back on the straightaways, or beginning to rise up out of the classic "sitting" position, that means he's getting tired. His time will suffer from such form breaks.

At many meets, spectators are allowed to stand along the outside of the mats. If you're near the starting line, cover your ears when the gun goes off. One of the best vantage points is at the top of the backstretch of the oval. From there, you can see the coaches skating along the outside of the track shouting instructions and displaying time boards to inform the skaters of their lap splits. Because this spot on the track is about 100 meters after the finish line, you'll be able to see each skater's and coach's reaction as a race ends. Wherever you are, usually you can take photographs or videotapes of the action if you want. Flash photography often is prohibited because it distracts the skaters.

Watching a Pack-Style Meet

Pack-style meets generally are low-key affairs. Most don't even charge admission. Spectators can stand right along the mats for a "coach's eye" view of the racing. Every skater will appreciate applause and a supportive cheer.

4

Getting Involved

Speed skating is an excellent way to help children develop balance and coordination, two keys to success in many other sports. While skating is a lifetime sport, it certainly is easier to master at a younger age than as an adult.

The best way to get started is to visit an ice rink in your area. It's not necessary to search out a coach for one-on-one instruction. Group lessons are less costly and often more fun. Practically

An official helps young skaters get set on the starting line.

every rink offers a learn-to-skate program designed to get you on your feet and give you the confidence to move around the rink. Such classes typically run several weeks and include both on-ice instruction and practice time. Ask about an introductory speed skating class to get lessons specifically aimed at speed skating.

Cy White / PHOTO ACTION USA

Masters skater Bob Norberg
takes the starting position.

Finding a Club

Ask, too, if there's a speed skating club at your rink. There are nearly 100 clubs in 19 state and regional associations throughout the United States, plus clubs that are not part of any association. The largest clubs and associations are in Wisconsin, Illinois, and Michigan, but you also can find clubs in California, Florida, Oklahoma, Texas, and other warmer-climate areas. The newest association serves skaters in the Las Vegas area. You don't have to be an Olympic hopeful to join.

A club will provide you with the instruction, information, and encouragement you need to improve. Clubs include skaters of all age groups and at many skill levels. You'll soon discover that speed skating clubs are full of friendly families who have been involved for years. They love to talk about their sport, so don't be shy with your questions.

If you need help finding a club, contact the *Amateur Speedskating Union*, which organizes competitions for skaters of all ages. Olympic and other international skating for American athletes is governed by a second organization, *US Speedskating*. The two organizations will merge effective March 2002 and will operate under the name US Speedskating. Olympic and other world competition is run by the International Skating Union, headquartered in Lausanne, Switzerland.

Switching from Another Sport

A fair number of U.S. athletes come into speed skating after participating in other ice sports. For instance, world speed skating champions Eric Heiden and Eric Flaim played hockey as kids, and Karen Cashman was a New England figure skating champion before winning an Olympic speed skating medal in 1994. So if you have any experience in hockey or figure skating, you're already on your way to learning how to speed skate.

The past few years have seen an influx of inline skaters onto the ice. While the technique isn't exactly the same, it's similar enough to give you a head start learning to speed skate. In fact, KC Boutiette qualified for the 1994 Olympic team only two months after he first took to the ice, an astonishing feat! Boutiette was joined by three other former inliners on the 1998 Olympic team. Some rinks are beginning to hold special classes for inliners who want to try speed skating on the ice. Another source of encouragement for inliners who want to try ice skating is a magazine called *Fitness and Speed Skating Times* (see Chapter 12)

A Broad Base of Competition

Children as young as three race in local "tiny tots" events, and U.S. National and North American competition is available for athletes in seven distinct divisions from age eight on up. The seventh division, the "Masters" category, is further subdivided into five age groups: 30–39, 40–49, 50–59, 60–69, and 70-plus.

In some areas, local park districts sponsor speed skating races on a frozen pond or lake, or at a hockey rink. Also, your neighborhood Boys & Girls Club may offer a program. Participating in or preparing a report about speed skating can help you earn a Girl Scout or Boy Scout sports merit badge; check with your troop leader for specific requirements. Someday, middle schools and high schools may offer speed skating as a competitive sport.

State Games

A great option for newcomers is the State Games program, which emphasizes sports development and participation at the grassroots level. State Games competitions usually are held on one or more weekends in a locale that can support a variety of ice and snow sports. To add an authentic flavor, some feature a torch-lighting ceremony with a former Olympic athlete. Wisconsin's program, known as the Badger State Games, is the nation's largest Winter Games. It had nearly 100 speed skaters (and more than 6,400 participants in all sports) in 2001, its 13th year of existence.

Nearly every state that has speed skating on its Winter Games schedule has short-track racing at an indoor hockey rink. The Utah Winter Games has both short- and long-track competitions—the recreational or beginning athlete's chance to skate on the lightning-quick 400-meter Utah Olympic Oval just outside Salt Lake City.

Surprisingly, Colorado, Minnesota, Michigan, and several other cold-weather states don't have Winter Games at all (as of 2001). And of the 16 states that do offer Winter Games, not all include speed skating. Some states don't offer Winter Games or speed skating because they haven't heard from enough people who want to enter or officiate. You can get involved! Contact your State Games organization to express your interest as a competitor or volunteer. The National Congress of State Games can help you hook up with the right people, or you can contact your governor's office or state tourism bureau.

If you can speed skate in your state's Winter Games, do check ahead for dates and other specific information. As of winter 2001, the following states conducted Winter State Games:

Arizona	Grand Canyon State Games	mid-late Feb., early March
California	California State Games	late Feb.
Idaho	Idaho Winter Games	late Jan., late Feb.
Iowa	Iowa Games	early Feb.
Kentucky	Bluegrass State Games	mid-March
Massachusetts	Bay State Games	late Jan., mid-Feb.

Nebraska	Cornhusker State Games	early Feb.
New Hampshire	Granite State Festival	early Feb.
New York	Empire State Games	late Feb.
Oklahoma	Sooner State Games	all Jan., early Feb.
Oregon	State Games of Oregon	early March
Pennsylvania	Keystone State Games	all Feb., early March, early April
Rhode Island	Rhode Island State Games	mid-Feb.
Utah	Utah Winter Games	all Jan.
Wisconsin	Badger State Games	early Feb.
Wyoming	Cowboy State Games	mid-Feb.

Challenged Athletes

With a few modifications, athletes with disabilities can enjoy speed skating. For instance, a person who uses supportive foot or ankle splints could wear them in her skates. Another type of special equipment makes skating comparable to wheelchair racing in the Summer Paralympics or the Boston Marathon. The athlete is seated on a sled, known as an *ice sledge*, that is equipped with skating-style blades. He uses special

Cy White / PHOTO ACTION USA

Special Olympics athlete Lynn Turner enjoys speed skating. Helping her is Erik Winberg.

poles to propel and steer himself around a standard 400-meter ice oval. Ice sledge racing is not part of the Salt Lake 2002 Paralympic schedule, but ice sledge hockey is.

The crowded, often chaotic conditions of short-track racing would make it extremely difficult and dangerous for a visually impaired person to compete. Yet a deaf skater could compete in long-track skating nearly as easily as do hearing athletes.

Cy White / PHOTO ACTION USA

Volunteers are a great help in teaching young skaters.

The day may not be far off when an athlete with a disability rises to the ranks of the speed skating elite.

At present, the most comprehensive program for speed skaters with disabilities can be found in the Special Olympics organization. Besides Special Olympics-specific competitions, athletes with cognitive challenges can participate in the "special needs" division of many local competitions. Check ahead with the meet director for specific rules.

Volunteers

One of the best things about speed skating is that it's a small sport in comparison to most others in the Olympic movement. Volunteer help is essential to the success of every meet. Many former speed skaters stay involved in the sport as coaches, rink guards, instructors, meet referees, starters, judges, and lap counters.

If you don't skate but have specialized qualifications, such as medical training or experience working as a timer at track or swim meets, your skills will be put to good use. Even if you have no sports experience, you can assist at the registration table, hand out pairing sheets, sell programs, work as an usher, or phone in results to the local newspaper. If you call a local club or event director and offer to help, you'll be welcomed warmly. And who knows, the volunteer right alongside you could be a former—or future—gold medalist.

Cy White / PHOTO ACTION USA

Four-time Olympic medalist Dianne
Holum pours water to repair the ice at a
short-track meet.

Speed Skating Associations

Amateur Speedskating Union of the United States (ASU)
Karen Kostal
Executive Director/Treasurer
OS 651 Forest St.
Winfield, IL 60190-1541
phone: (800) 634-4766 or (630) 784-8662
fax: (630) 784-8667
Internet: http://www.speed skating.org/
e-mail: ASUkostal@aol.com

In 2001 the ASU had about 2,000 members in five membership categories. Brochures and other materials are available.

Ice Skating Institute (ISI)
17120 N. Dallas Pkwy., Suite 140
Dallas, TX 75248
phone: (972) 735-8800
fax: (972) 735-8815
Internet: http://www.skateisi.com/
e-mail: isi@skateisi.org

Many rinks around the country are affiliated with the ISI for the purpose of standardizing classes and testing. The ISI offers a test sheet and speed skating patches for five ability levels. No speed skating publications are available through the ISI.

US Speedskating
Katie Marquard, Executive Director
PO Box 450639
Westlake, OH 44145
phone: (440) 899-0128
fax: (440) 899-0109

Internet: http://www.usspeedskating.org/
e-mail: usskate@ix.netcom.com

US Speedskating has been the national governing body for Olympic and international racing since 1966. It will take over the ASU's role in developing skaters when the two organizations merge in March 2002.

International Skating Union (ISU)
Chemin de Primerose 2
CH 1007
Lausanne, Switzerland
phone: (+41) 21 612 66 66
fax: (+41) 21 612 66 77
Internet: http://www.isu.org/
e-mail: info@isu.ch

Other Sports Associations

International Olympic Committee (IOC)
Chateau de Vidy
Case Postale 356
1007 Lausanne, Switzerland
phone: (+41) 21 621 61 11
fax: (+41) 21 621 6216
Internet: http://www.olympic.org

United States Olympic Committee (USOC)
One Olympic Plaza
Colorado Springs, CO 80909-5760
phone: (719) 632-5551
fax: (719) 578-4654
Internet: http://www.usolympicteam.com

National Congress of State Games
PO Box 7136
Billings, MT 59103
phone: (406) 254-7426
fax: (406) 254-7439
Internet: http://www.stategames.org/sgoa/
e-mail: stori@stategames.org

Organizing Committees

Salt Lake Organizing Committee
299 S. Main St., Suite 1300
PO Box 45002
Salt Lake City, UT 84145
ph. (801) 322-2002
fax: (801) 364-7644
Internet: http://www.saltlake2002.com
(Feb. 8-24, 2002)

Salt Lake Paralympic Organizing Committee
PO Box 45002
Salt Lake City, UT 84145
phone: (801) 322-2002
fax: (801) 364-7644
Internet: http://www.saltlake2002.com
(March 7-16, 2002)

Torino 2006 Organizing Committee
Turin, Italy
http://www.torino2006.it/eng
(Feb. 11-26, 2006)

Sports Organizations for Athletes with Disabilities

Special Olympics International
1325 G St., NW, Suite 500
Washington, DC 20005
phone: (202) 628-3630
fax: (202) 824-0200
Internet: http://www.specialolympics.org
e-mail: SOImail@aol.com

Approximately 11,000 athletes compete in Special Olympics speed skating worldwide. The events range from a 25-meter straightaway race for beginners and skaters of lower ability to the 1,500 meters. Special Olympians can partner with peer athletes without mental disabilities in "Unified Sports" races and relays. Several prominent speed skating clubs have partnerships with local Special Olympics groups to share coaching expertise.

Wheelchair Sports, USA
3595 E. Fountain Blvd., Suite L-1
Colorado Springs, CO 80910
phone: (719) 574-1150
fax: (719) 574-9840
Internet: www.wsusa.org
e-mail: wsusa@aol.com

Wheelchair Sports plans to launch competition in ice-sledge racing once interest in the events has been identified.

United States Association of Blind Athletes
33 N. Institute St.
Colorado Springs, CO 80903
phone: (719) 630-0422
fax: (719) 630-0616
Internet: http://www.usaba.org
e-mail: media@usaba.org

While speed skating is not offered by the USABA, a spokeswoman says the organization is interested in assisting blind and visually impaired athletes who wish to pursue the sport.

United States Cerebral Palsy Athletic Association
25 W. Independence Way
Kingston, RI 02881
phone: (401) 792-7130
fax: (401) 792-7132
Internet: http://www.uscpaa.org
e-mail: uscpaa@mail.bbsnet.com

Disabled Sports USA
451 Hungerford Dr., Suite 100
Rockville, MD 20850
phone: (301) 217-0960
fax: (301) 217-0968
TTD: (301) 217-0963
Internet: http://www.dsusa.org
e-mail: information@dsusa.org

Dwarf Athletic Association of America
418 Willow Way
Lewisville, TX 75067
phone: (972) 317-8299
fax: (972) 966-0184
Internet: http://www.daaa.org/
e-mail: Daaa@flash.net

USA Deaf Sports Federation
3607 Washington Blvd., Suite 4
Ogden, UT 84403-1737
phone: (801) 393-8710
fax: (801) 393-2263
TTY: (801) 393-7916
Internet: http://www.usadsf.org/
e-mail: homeoffice@usadsf.org

The above four organizations do not list speed skating among their programs. The contact information is included as a courtesy to the reader.

400-meter Speed Skating Ovals in the United States

Enclosed Ovals

Pettit National Ice Center
500 S. 84th St.
Milwaukee WI 53214
phone: (414) 266-0100
fax: (414) 266-0122
Internet: www.thepettit.com
e-mail: info@thepettit.com

Utah Olympic Oval
5662 S. 4800 West
Kearns, UT 84118
phone: (801) 968-OVAL
fax: (801) 963-7112
Internet: www.saltlake2002.com (until May 2002)
www.utaholympicoval.com (after May 2002)
e-mail: utaholympicoval@saltlake2002.com

Outdoor Ovals

John Rose Oval
2661 Civic Center Dr.
Roseville, MN 55113
phone: (651) 415-2160
fax: (651) 415-2171
Internet: http://www.ci.roseville.mn.us/oval/
e-mail: ericr@rernet.org

Sheffield Speed Skating Oval
218 Main St.
Lake Placid, NY 12946
phone: (518) 523-1655
fax: (518) 523-5366
Internet: http://www.orda.org/ocpubskate.html
e-mail: mstanton@orda.org

United States High Altitude Sports Center
Continental Drive Interchange on Interstate 90
PO Box 3208
Butte, MT 59701
phone: (406) 494-7570 (winter)
phone: (406) 497-2832 (summer)

5

Skating
Fundamentals

Ready to give speed skating a try?

If you've never stood on a pair of ice skates, the very idea of lacing up a pair with long blades, bending over like you're in an old Groucho Marx movie, and propelling yourself around the rink sounds impossible—even absurd. But just as a child learns to stand before learning to walk, an aspiring speed skater needs to become comfortable with the basic skating position before getting on the ice.

You'll quickly see why skaters brag about how low they can *sit*. The lower the skating position, the farther

Cy White / PHOTO ACTION USA

A future Olympian?

to the side the skater can push each stroke, generating more speed. Another benefit of a low skating position is that it's more aerodynamic than skating upright.

The Basic Position

The best way to learn the skating position is in your sneakers, in front of a full-length mirror. Here are the basics:

- Stand with your feet about six inches apart.
- Hold your arms at your sides, bent at the elbows at a 90-degree angle.
- Begin bending the knees, as if you are lowering yourself into a chair.
- Keeping the 90-degree angle in your arms, pull your arms in front of you. Your fingertips should be pointed ahead of you, and your thumbs should be on top.
- Bend forward at the waist until you can rest your forearms on your thighs.
- Keep your buttocks down and your head up. A slightly rounded back is OK.

You can practice this position in your living room. Pay attention to the particular muscle groups affected. Chapter 8 features some additional suggestions.

Weight Shifting

Now you're ready to learn how to shift from one foot to the other and back again. In the position described above, lean slightly to one side, enough to rest both forearms on the same thigh. Keep your other foot flat on the floor. You'll feel your body weight being supported by one leg. That becomes your *support leg*. Your *pushing leg* relaxes because it's not bearing any weight. Now shift to the opposite side. By repeating the weight shift, you begin to get the feel for how you'll balance on one skate on the ice.

Cy White / PHOTO ACTION USA

Mike Gallant practices technique on a slide board.

If you are proficient at basic ice skating or inline skating, you may already know how to balance on one foot on skates. When you take to the ice in speed skates, there's no point in practicing your weight shift in a standing position; instead, you should assume the proper speed skating stance. One reason for this is that it's critical to get your legs and back muscles working properly. Another good reason to be in the speed skating position when you work on weight shifting is that if you do lose your balance and topple over, you're already low to the ice and rolled up in a ball. It's almost impossible to break a wrist in a fall like that.

Stroking

The next important lesson is how to stroke on the ice. There are two phases to the stroke: the push and the glide. With your weight centered, begin to push one foot directly to the side. During this push, you are shifting your weight to the support leg. Ideally, you'll be sitting low and extending your push as far to the side as possible. At the end of the push, your pushing leg will release from the ice and you'll be gliding on your support leg. Let your free foot fall back behind you for a couple of seconds, then set it down on the ice again, next to the other foot and about a half boot-length ahead. Switch feet and repeat.

At first, of course, you won't be moving at world-record speeds. Your goal is to learn the rhythm of the skating technique. A good goal to set for yourself at this point is skating quietly (unless you are using clap skates). If you hear a scratching sound as you push, that means you're pushing with the toes of your blades instead of with the flat of the blade.

Arm Swing

Now it's time to get your arms working for you. Good arm swing technique helps you move down the ice. As with stroking, there are two phases to this part of speed skating technique: *forward swing* and *rear swing*.

When your arm swings forward, it should be bent slightly, with your thumb on top. Don't swing above shoulder height. Your hand should slightly cross midline—this helps you shift your weight. Maintain the slight bend in your elbow; there's no need to bring your hand any closer than six inches from your chin.

The rear arm swing is simple. Let your arm swing straight backward, parallel to the body, until it is even with or slightly higher than your back.

Later, as your legs get stronger and you're skating more laps, you'll want to conserve energy by skating with one or both arms resting on your back on the straightaways. You'll continue to swing at least one arm when skating the corners.

Cy White / PHOTO ACTION USA

Chris Witty shows proper arm
swings while skating turns.

Crossovers

To negotiate the turns and stay close to the inside of your lane,
you'll need to learn *crossover* steps. The basics of push and glide
apply here, with one key difference: instead of setting your right
foot down next to your left, you must cross it over. This can be
tricky when your skate blades are nearly one and one-half feet
long! Step slightly ahead of your left instep.

Skating crossovers requires extra flexibility in your hips and lower back. Crossovers also require you to be in control of the edges of your skate blades. As your right foot crosses over, let your left foot roll slightly so you can push with the outside edge of the blade.

Some instructors have their classes walk through the crossover technique while holding onto the rinkside mats or boards. This is a good way to help you see where your feet need to be going.

Besides skating crossover steps, you'll also need to adjust your arm swing on the turns. The arms, bent at a 90-degree angle, swing across the body more. The rear swing phase is less pronounced.

Cy White / PHOTO ACTION USA

Mary Mane Maierle demonstrates to Jacob
Bolware how to cross the right foot over the left.

Stopping

Among the acceptable options are the snowplow stop (knees bent, toes pointed inward) and the modified hockey stop (twist at the waist and shift your weight onto your rear foot). You'll also see some skaters drag a toe to slow themselves, but that's frowned upon because it unnecessarily gouges the ice. Beginners may find it easiest simply to coast to a stop.

6

Skates

Figure Skate

Hockey Skate

Short-Track Speed Skate
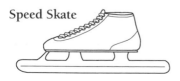

Speed Skate

Watch hockey players or figure skaters and you'll see some slick skating. But to really move on the ice, it takes a pair of speed skates. Speed skates have extra-long blades, extending a couple of inches beyond the toe and heel of the boot. By powerfully pushing the long blade against the ice, speed skaters move much faster than hockey players, figure skaters, or even the world's best runners. Typically, women's blades average about 16 inches and men's about 17 inches—far longer than those on hockey or figure skates, in part because speed skaters don't need to make sudden stops or changes of direction.

Typically, beginners' skates come with blades, although some people prefer to buy boots separately and install blades from another manufacturer. Long-track boots are made of leather, while short-track specialists wear boots that are custom-molded to the foot and reinforced in the ankles. The blades on short-track skates are affixed slightly off-center to aid the skater in leaning into the tight corners.

Getting a Good Fit

People who haven't tried ice skating often say they'll never master the sport because they have "weak ankles." But skating instructors and coaches will tell you there's no such thing as weak ankles—just poorly fitting skates that don't sufficiently support the ankles.

If you're just starting out in speed skating, the first thing you'll need to figure out is your skate size. Many models of speed skates are made outside the United States, so sizes will be different. For instance, a woman's American size 6 is equivalent to a European size 37 skate.

Don't just guess at your size. Have your feet measured. Parents should avoid the temptation to buy skates a child can "grow into." If the boot doesn't fit snugly, a youngster will never feel completely confident on skates.

Another trap to avoid is wearing two pairs of socks, or wearing socks that are too heavy. Your skates will fit better (and you'll avoid painful blisters) if you wear one good-quality pair of thin socks. Many top skaters say that by skipping socks altogether, they have a better feel for the ice. If you'll be doing a lot of skating outdoors, invest in a set of boot covers to wear over your skates for added warmth.

Rent or Buy?

To keep your costs low as you begin speed skating, you may want to see whether your rink rents speed skates on a daily basis. The cost of renting for a weekly class and a few practices will add up quickly, however. When you're ready to buy skates, check the bulletin board for a used pair in your size. Many rinks and speed skating clubs organize skate sales so people can buy used equipment at an affordable price.

If you're ready to make the investment in new skates, check out the pro shop. If you don't see what you need, a good pro shop manager will be happy to order skates for you. Mail order and online shopping are other options.

Clap Skates

Because Olympic medals are decided by hundredths of a second, skaters are always looking for ways to improve their times. A revolution in long-track speed skating took place in 1996 with the introduction of the clap skate, the first major technological innovation in speed skating equipment in more than 100 years. World-class skaters found that the use of clap skates cut about one second per lap from their times. Records weren't just broken—they were shattered!

Here's how the clap skate works. Instead of having the entire blade attached to the boot, the clap skate's blade is mounted to a spring-and-hinge mechanism at the front. The skater can lift her heel away from the blade, meaning that even as she completes

Clap Skate

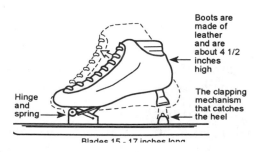

Boots are made of leather and are about 4 1/2 inches high

Hinge and spring

The clapping mechanism that catches the heel

Blades 15 - 17 inches long

each skating stroke and begins to pull her foot back in, her blade remains in contact with the ice a fraction of a second longer. It looks and sounds a little like a three-year-old clomping around in her mother's high heels. But since blade contact with the ice is what generates speed, the skating world has quickly become accustomed to the "clapping" sound as the blade snaps back into place. Just as baseball players need to break in their new gloves, skaters have had to become experts at tinkering with their blades until they are comfortable with the setup.

Although clap skates are designed for world-class athletes and are more costly and difficult to maintain than traditional skates, some youngsters and even recreational skaters are trying them. It will be interesting to see whether the clap skates replace the traditional models at all levels in the next few years.

Clap skates have not been widely used in short-track racing because the crowded conditions put less of a premium on long, powerful stroking. In fact, the International Skating Union has banned their use in international competitions.

Sharpening Your Blades

Regardless of the type of speed skates you choose, you'll have to learn how to sharpen the blades. You may have seen a professional skate sharpener working on hockey or figure skates. An electric-powered sharpening wheel is needed because hockey and figure skate blades feature a groove down the center. But speed skate blades have a flat edge, and even kids can learn to sharpen their own by rubbing a special *stone* across them. This is done while the skates are in a *jig*, a special rack that holds the skates level, with the blades facing upward. A jig is lightweight (usually made of aluminum) and about the size of a shoe box, so it's easy to transport. Competitive skaters sharpen their skates between races.

Once your blades are sharpened, you'll want to keep them from being scratched or banged around in your gear bag. Use plastic or leather *blade guards* to protect them. Even though it's just a few steps from the skate-changing bench to the ice, don't walk in your skates without blade guards—not even if the area is carpeted or covered by a rubber mat. Dirt, carpet fibers, or a shred of paper on your blades is all it takes to slow you down. Never, ever walk on a concrete floor in skates without sturdy blade guards.

Whether heading to the rink to work out or to race for a world championship, take extra care to pack everything you (and your skates) will need. Don't forget extra shoelaces in case one breaks. When flying to compete, take your skates and your skating clothing, etc., in a carry-on bag rather than checking these essentials with the airline.

Safety Concerns

You should be extra careful with your skates for safety's sake, too. It doesn't take much contact with a sharp blade to cut yourself or someone else. If your rink has a sports medicine clinic, let the pros there treat any cuts or other injuries. It's also a good idea to keep a small first-aid kit in your bag. A plastic bottle of liquid antiseptic, a few gauze pads, and a dozen adhesive bandages will easily fit in a zip-style sandwich bag. Be sure you properly dispose of any used gauze pads. (For more on safety and first aid, see Chapter 9.)

Blade Care

After skating, use your blade guards to get back to the bench, and remove your skates right away. Use an old towel to wipe the ice shavings off your blades, then put on knitted or stretch-terrycloth *blade covers*—they'll absorb any remaining moisture. Keep the cloth blade covers on until you get your skates home, then remove the covers to let the blades air-dry. Remember, polished steel blades will expand and contract slightly with changes in temperature, so don't keep tight-fitting blade guards on your skates when they're not in use. Your skates are your biggest and most important investment, so take good care of them!

7

Clothing and Accessories

The types of clothing and accessories necessary for speed skating depend on several factors. Are you a serious skater with Olympic aspirations? Are you a youngster just starting out, hoping to become skilled enough to compete? Or are you drawn to speed skating strictly as a fitness activity?

Comfort and safety dictate much of what a speed skater wears. Certainly, a novice doesn't need to outfit himself exactly like a world-class athlete. But once you know why the Olympians dress the way they do, you might want to consider making a larger investment in your skating apparel.

Clothing

While baggy jeans might suffice for casual figure skating or hockey, they'll never do for speed skating. If a skater were to catch his long speed skating blade in bulky fabric, he'd quickly fall to the ice—and probably take a few other skaters down with him!

For speed skating, you need something that moves with you. Wear snug warmup pants or exercise tights. You can find them on the fitness-wear racks at a department or sporting goods store,

Cy White / PHOTO ACTION USA

**Warm clothing is essential
in speed skating.**

or at specialty shops that carry clothing for cycling, running, or snow skiing. Synthetic fabrics are common; a synthetic/cotton blend provides a bit more warmth.

You may need to wear two or even three layers of clothing on your upper body. Your first layer should be a cotton turtleneck shirt; be sure it's plenty long and won't come untucked from your pants as you bend over. Next add a fleece sweatshirt and, if necessary, a nylon jacket to protect you from the wind and snow. For lengthier workouts on an outdoor rink, you might want your first layer to be made of a synthetic fabric that helps wick the sweat away from your skin. With this type of garment, you won't chill as easily.

The most important item in the wardrobe of a serious long-track skater is the *skin*, a tight-fitting, one-piece uniform. It's easy to see why it's called a skin—zipped up, the uniform is as snug as a second layer of skin, and it should be just as comfortable. Under the skin, skaters usually wear just a long- or short-sleeved T-shirt and underwear; most women wear a sports bra. For racing, long-track skaters wear a long-sleeved skin with an attached hood. The purpose of the hood is to hold the hair in place, keep the ears warm, and enhance the skater's aerodynamics. One of a skater's proudest moments is receiving his or her first team skin, whether representing a club in a local meet or the United States in an international competition.

Cy White / PHOTO ACTION USA

Bonnie Blair zips up
her skin before a race.

On practice days, many skaters opt for the freedom of movement afforded by a sleeveless, non-hooded skin over a T-shirt, topped by a favorite sweatshirt, and a warm headband or stocking cap. For outdoor skating or for warmup and cooldown laps at a competition, skaters typically add gloves or mittens and outer pants equipped with full-length side zippers. The full-length zippers allow the outer pants to be removed without taking off the skates.

As with skates, the fit of the skin is critical. A baggy skin is not only unattractive but also potentially dangerous; moreover, it won't help reduce wind resistance (which is the skin's main function). A skin that's too tight will be uncomfortable and probably will split when and where you least want it to. Whatever your skating outfit, pay close attention to the washing instructions and you'll prolong its life.

Eye Protection

Speed skaters almost never wear ordinary eyeglasses for corrective purposes. The combination of the skater's body heat and the air temperature can cause regular eyeglasses to fog up, so most skaters switch to contact lenses.

Because arm swing and arm position are an important part of technique, no speed skater wants to have to reach up to wipe water droplets (from flying ice shavings) or dust from the eyes. Many competitive skaters wear wraparound-style goggles with clear or tinted lenses to prevent eye problems that, although seemingly minor, might cause a fall in practice or cost valuable time in a race.

Goggles can be doubly helpful to a skater who wears contacts. The wind effect created by skating repeated laps can dry the eyes, making the lens uncomfortable or even causing it to pop out. In addition, the dehumidifying equipment designed to create optimal ice conditions at an indoor rink can contribute to a skater's dry-eye woes. Wearing goggles helps shield the contact lens user from both these potential problems.

Special Equipment for Short Track Skating

Cy White / PHOTO ACTION USA

Hillary Mills skates equipped for short-track.

The tight turns and crowded conditions of short-track skating call for special protective equipment. From time to time, the most experienced short-track skaters fall or are inadvertently kicked or tripped during a practice or race. Even though the dasher boards of the rink are covered with padding as thick as a mattress, a skater who skids into the wall without the right gear could be seriously hurt.

Starting from the skates up, short-trackers need to protect themselves from potential injury. They wear *shin guards* under their skin and *knee pads* over their skin, or a combination protective guard. Because short-track skaters commonly drag the left hand on the inside of the ice for balance, it makes sense for them to wear lightweight leather gloves. The gloves also ease the sting of a fall.

Of course, a fall can be extremely dangerous if a skater skids blades-first into other athletes. To protect against neck injuries and cuts to the throat, short-track skaters are required to wear neck protection. The skating skins worn in short-track racing are hoodless.

The whole outfit is topped off by a hard-shell *helmet* similar to a cycling helmet. In fact, beginning short-track skaters often use their bike helmets to reduce their costs. The key, of course, is to wear a helmet that fits snugly and to make sure that all the straps are properly secured.

Cy White / PHOTO ACTION USA

A short-track helmet fitting snugly on
the head of Nick Pearson

8

Fitness and Nutrition

Whether you skate for exercise or on a competitive basis, you'll enjoy yourself more and get better results if you are physically fit. That means getting yourself in shape, stretching, eating right, getting the proper amount of sleep, and staying away from alcohol and other drugs.

Off-Ice Training

Building strength and endurance in your legs and back muscles is essential to successful and enjoyable speed skating. Cycling is an excellent way to achieve the fitness you need. When you bend over to grasp turned-down, racing-style handlebars, your back is in a position very similar to that of a speed skater's. Not only does cycling strengthen your heart and improve your aerobic capacity, but pedaling a bike also gets your legs used to repetitive motion.

It should come as no surprise that some of the very best speed skaters can also compete at a world-class level in cycling. Chris Witty was an alternate to the 1996 Olympic cycling team; at Sydney in 2000 she placed fifth in the 500-meter time trial. Another success story is that of Connie Carpenter Phinney, who

Cy White / PHOTO ACTION USA

Bonnie Blair does
off-ice training.

skated in the 1972 Games and later won a gold medal for the U.S. in cycling in the Los Angeles Olympics.

Running is another way to strengthen your heart and legs for skating. For the greatest benefit, run up hills using short, choppy steps. You also can bend over into the skating position and *low walk* to isolate the muscles used in skating. Advanced skaters use *plyometric jumps* to improve their explosiveness. It's best to have a coach direct you in advanced exercises to avoid poor posture or technique that actually could hinder your progress or result in injury.

Weightlifting is another common *dry-land* training tool for advanced skaters. Among the most-used techniques are squats, lunges, and various abdominal and back exercises. One of the major benefits of weight training is its effect on the back. Experts say the weights used should be light enough so that you don't need to wear a support belt; after all, the point is to build the muscles that stabilize the hips and lower back. Weightlifting isn't for the beginning skater, and it should never be incorporated into a training plan without the supervision of a qualified instructor.

Even before inline skating took hold as a major fitness activity, speed skaters used roller skating as an off-season training method. For instance, Eric and Beth Heiden prepared for their 1980 Olympic medals by working out during the summers on early-model inlines in Madison, Wisconsin. With design improvements coming rapidly in both inline and ice skates, many top speed skaters now wear boots that can accommodate either a set of wheels or a steel skating blade. Obviously, custom-made skating boots are more costly than off-the-shelf models. You may want to check a better inline retailer for skates with five wheels and low-cut boots similar to speed skates.

If you choose cycling or inline skating to supplement your on-ice work, be sure to select your training site with local ordinances, traffic laws, and vehicle volume in mind. Always wear appropriate safety gear, such as a helmet or wrist guards. Olympic skater Moira D'Andrea credited a helmet with saving her life in a serious bicycle accident in 1996.

Stretching

It's important to stretch both before and after each workout or race. Besides the obvious physical benefits, stretching also gives you time to review your workout plan or clear your head before competition. Find a quiet spot away from other people: it's tough to focus on proper stretching technique when you're carrying on a conversation. You'll see a lot of skaters listening to music— wearing headphones is a great way to tell the world you don't want to be bothered at the moment.

Consult a physical therapist or other medical expert for specific tips on techniques and recommended repetitions for your fitness level. With all types of stretching, the goal is to produce a comfortable stretch, not a painful one. And remember—don't bounce or jerk.

The hamstrings, hips, buttocks, and calves are areas that all need attention. Don't forget about strengthening the neck muscles so you can maintain good form on the ice. After all, you won't be able to see where you're going if you're not holding your head up.

Spinal Stretch

The Amateur Speedskating Union suggests this exercise: Sit with right leg extended. Bend left leg and cross it over right, placing foot flat on the ground next to outside of right knee. Left hand can be placed behind you for stability. Turn slowly to look over left shoulder. Turn upper body, but not hips. Breathe easily. Hold stretch five seconds, relax, and turn back to face front. Do this stretch in sets of three on each side.

Nutrition

Following a balanced diet regimen makes sense no matter what sport you engage in. A good workout or race requires "fuel" the same way a car needs gasoline. A good starting point in planning your diet is the following list of daily recommendations from the U.S. Department of Agriculture:

- 6 to 11 servings of grain
- 3 to 5 servings of vegetables
- 2 to 4 servings of fruit
- 2 to 3 servings of dairy products
- 5 to 7 ounces of meat

Even though some races last less than a minute, speed skaters need plenty of energy for practices and competition. Pasta is a great source of carbohydrates—the food your body turns into energy. So it's no surprise that many of America's top skaters say their favorite foods are spaghetti and lasagna. However, you won't want a heavy meal in your system when you're skating. You'll perform better if you don't feel full or bloated. The time for a big meal is the night before a competition, or on days when you're not working out.

If you'll be practicing or competing in the morning, you should eat a moderate breakfast a couple of hours before you hit the ice. Before an afternoon workout or race, you might want to eat a

A Guide to Daily Food Choic

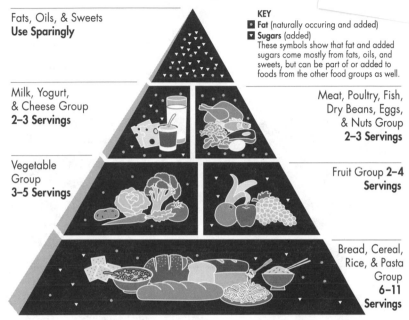

Fats, Oils, & Sweets
Use Sparingly

KEY
◼ **Fat** (naturally occuring and added)
▾ **Sugars** (added)
These symbols show that fat and added sugars come mostly from fats, oils, and sweets, but can be part of or added to foods from the other food groups as well.

Milk, Yogurt,
& Cheese Group
2–3 Servings

Meat, Poultry, Fish,
Dry Beans, Eggs,
& Nuts Group
2–3 Servings

Vegetable
Group
3–5 Servings

Fruit Group **2–4
Servings**

Bread, Cereal,
Rice, & Pasta
Group
**6–11
Servings**

Source: U.S. Department of Agriculture and the
U.S. Department of Health and Human Services

hearty breakfast and a lighter lunch, such as a bowl of soup. A small snack 30 to 60 minutes before you begin skating is fine— but you should stay away from pretzels or other salty snacks. In fact, avoiding "junk food" is a good idea at all times. Olympic champion Bonnie Blair found that a peanut butter-and-jelly sandwich a couple of hours before a race settled her stomach! Other skaters munch on fresh fruit or bread when they have to race several times in one day.

After a workout or your last race of the day, it's important to replenish your energy stores. Experts recommend about 300 calories of carbohydrates within an hour after activity. Among your choices are carbohydrate-replacement sports drinks—the grocery stores are full of them—and bagels and potatoes. Not only will you quiet your growling stomach, but you'll also be preparing your body for the next day's races or practice.

Keeping Hydrated

Remember to keep your body well hydrated. Even when you're skating outdoors during winter or in a cool ice rink, you can still work up a good sweat. Indoor rinks are a low-humidity environment, so sweat can evaporate before you even realize it's there.

Cy White / PHOTO ACTION USA

Bonnie Blair and Chris Witty both drink water after racing.

Don't start your workout or race thirsty, but don't drink so much that you need to use the bathroom the minute you lace up your skates. A good rule of thumb is to drink four to eight ounces every 20 to 30 minutes during a practice or meet. Within the first two hours after exercise, drink at least 16 ounces. A smart skater makes filling a sports bottle as much a part of her pre-skating routine as packing her skates.

But what to drink? Experts recommend sports drinks or water. You'll want to avoid fizzy mineral waters and soft drinks before and during your ice time. The carbonation might upset your stomach, particularly because of the time you'll spend in the bent-over skating position. Fruit juices and soft drinks should be diluted by half to provide the proper percentage of carbohydrates. And remember, caffeine-free soft drinks are preferred because caffeine can slow down the body's absorption of fluids.

Sleep

Be sure you're getting enough sleep. It's tough to concentrate on your training plan or race pace when you're yawning. Statistics show that athletes who are tired are more likely to become injured.

It's only natural to be a little restless the night before a big race, so try to get your normal number of hours of sleep in the two or three nights before competition. Remember also that proper rest means lying quietly without reading or watching television. Your brain needs a break, too!

Alcohol and Other Drugs

No young athlete should drink alcohol, smoke, or misuse drugs. These substances can lead to all sorts of problems. Ask yourself: will what you're putting into your body make you a better athlete or not?

Athletes who become involved in the upper levels of competition are subject to random drug tests. The object of these tests is to weed out unethical individuals who would use steroids or other performance-enhancing drugs. However, many types of common medicines, including some used for colds and allergies, also are prohibited because of their complex chemistry or because they can mask the presence of banned substances.

A violation of the anti-drug rules can have very serious consequences, including losing your spot on the Olympic team. Athletes, parents, and coaches with drug-related questions can phone the U.S. Anti-Doping Agency Drug Reference Line (1-800-233-0393) or go to the USADA's web site: http:// www.usantidoping.org/.

9

Safety and First Aid

Speed skating safety cannot be overemphasized. No one ever wants to see an athlete get hurt. Many speed skating injuries can be avoided through a proper medical examination, correct flexibility training, and appropriate physical conditioning. Since all athletes do get bumps and bruises—and, occasionally, more serious injuries—here are a few precautions to keep in mind at practices and competitions:

- Wear the right clothes for practice sessions.
- Leave any jewelry—watches, rings, earrings, etc.—in your locker or in a duffel bag. This rule applies to boys as well as girls.
- Stow equipment in one area off the ice.
- Go through a warmup session and do stretching exercises before the practice begins. This prevents muscle strains and aches and pains.
- Skip a practice if you are not feeling well. Recovery will be quicker than if you had practiced or competed while under the weather.
- Drink plenty of water. Dehydration can occur quickly. Don't wait until you are thirsty to get a drink. Some coaches recommended sports drinks and think they are useful, but water is just as good, if not better.

The First Aid Kit

Injuries go hand-in-hand with sports. It's wise to know what to do to handle the inevitable bumps, bruises, and scrapes, along with more serious injuries. A well-stocked first aid kit should include:

• Adhesive bandages in different shapes and sizes
• Adhesive tape in different sizes
• Ammonia caps for dizziness
• Antiseptic soap for washing a wound area
• Antiseptic solution for minor scrapes
• Aspirin, or its equivalent, for simple headaches. (Remember: For youth teams, no medication should be given without written permission from a doctor or guardian, signed and dated, authorizing the disbursement of aspirin or other medication.)
• Blanket to cover an injured athlete, since warmth reduces the chance of shock
• Cold packs
• Disposable towels
• Elastic wraps of various sizes
• Eyewash solution
• Gauze pads
• Hank's solution for a knocked-out tooth (trade name Save-A-Tooth®)
• Plastic bottle filled with fresh water
• Scissors and an eyedropper
• Sterile cotton sheets that can be cut to fit
• Tissues and premoistened towelettes
• Tweezers

Remember that Occupational Safety and Health Administration (OSHA) regulations must be followed when disposing of any items that have blood contamination.

It is a good idea to have a list of emergency telephone numbers taped inside the first aid kit, but in a real emergency, dial 911. Be sure to keep some spare change in the first aid kit to use with a pay telephone.

Treating Injuries and Other Problems

Many large competitions have a physician, nurse, or other trained health care professional on hand to take care of any serious injury. However, you should never assume that precautions have been taken. Check in advance to be sure. Always be prepared. Proper planning prevents problems.

In coping with a serious injury, coaches may find the following guidelines helpful:

- Always remain calm. Don't panic or appear flustered. Others around you will take their behavior cues from you.
- Don't try to be a doctor. When in doubt about the severity of an injury, send the athlete to a physician, or let the on-site physician, nurse, or other health care professional make the decision.
- Never move a skater who has a serious injury. Don't try to make the injured person more comfortable by moving the skater off the ice or into the locker room. This can make a serious injury worse. Be safe, not sorry, and call in the designated professionals if you have doubts about an injury. Under no circumstances should an unconscious speed skater be moved. Stay with the skater until a professional arrives.

Scrapes and Burns

Wash scrapes and burns with an antiseptic cleaning solution and cover with sterile gauze. This is usually all that is needed to promote quick healing of these common injuries.

Blisters

Blisters are fairly common problems for speed skaters. Well-fitting skates can go a long way toward preventing these annoying, painful injuries. Any blisters that do occur should be kept clean and covered with a bandage, especially if the blister breaks. Over-the-counter medications to treat blisters are available, but whenever possible the skater should follow the doctor's or coach's suggestions.

Cuts

Small cuts need pressure to slow the bleeding. After the bleeding slows, wash the area with an antiseptic solution, cover with sterile gauze taped in place, and continue to apply pressure. Of course, any deep cut or large gash may need stitches, so the injured skater should see a doctor as soon as possible.

Communicable Diseases

Communicable diseases such as boils, athlete's foot, ringworm, and cold sores are common afflictions among speed skaters. Mouth sores may be treated with over-the-counter medication, but the skater should check with a coach or doctor before using any of these. The best medicine, however, is prevention. Speed skaters should avoid using other skaters' equipment, and should make sure to keep their own equipment clean.

Muscle Pulls, Sprains, and Bruises

Rest, ice, compression, and elevation (RICE) are the steps needed to handle these injuries and are about all you should do in the way of treatment. RICE reduces the swelling of most injuries and helps speed recovery.

After an injury, the coach should have the injured skater stop and rest. Apply ice, compress with an elastic bandage, and elevate the injured arm, leg, knee, or ankle. Ice reduces swelling and

Cy White / PHOTO ACTION USA

German skater Mathias Pfeifer loses his edge,
crashing into the protective pads on a curve.

pain, and should be left on the injured area until it becomes
uncomfortable. When that happens, remove the ice pack and let
the injured skater rest for 15 minutes, then reapply. These are the
immediate steps to take until a doctor arrives.

Over the next few days, the injury should be treated with two to
three 20-minute icing sessions per day at two and one-half hour
intervals. This should provide noticeable improvement. Don't overdo
the icing; 20 minutes is long enough. In most cases, after two or
three days, or when the swelling has been significantly reduced,
heat can be applied in the form of warm-water soaks. Fifteen minutes
of warm soaking, along with a gradual return to motion, will speed
the healing process.

Another approach after two or three days, if the doctor agrees, is
to begin motion, strength, and alternative (MSA) exercise. The
American Institute for Preventive Medicine recommends:

- *Motion*: Moving the injured area and reestablishing a range of motion.
- *Strength*: Working to increase the strength of the injured area once any inflammation subsides and the range of motion begins to return.
- *Alternative*: Regularly performing an alternative exercise that does not stress the injury.

Seek the advice of a sports-medicine professional prior to starting any treatment plan. Specially shaped pads are useful for knee and ankle injuries, and they can be used in combination with ice, compression, and elevation. For a simple bruise, apply an ice pack.

Head Injuries

Blows to the upper part of the head, especially near the eye, can cause bleeding under the skin and result in a black eye. An ice pack applied to the area will reduce the swelling until a doctor can evaluate the injury.

Normally, the eye can wash out most foreign particles because of its ability to produce tears. If this doesn't work, use an eye-cleaning solution to wash out the irritant. Here are a few simple guidelines a skater can follow when dealing with an eye irritant:

- Don't rub the eye or use anything dirty, such as a cloth or a finger, to remove the irritant.
- With clean hands, pull the eyelid forward and down as you look at the floor.
- Flush with eyewash, or use a clean, sterile cloth to remove any particle you see in the eye.

If the foreign object remains, the coach should cover the eye with a clean gauze pad and have the athlete visit a doctor.

Nosebleeds usually don't last very long. A speed skater with a nosebleed should sit quietly and apply a cold pack to the bridge of the nose, while pinching the nostril at its base.

A knocked-out tooth can be successfully replanted if it is stored and transported properly. The tooth should be placed in a transport container with a solution such as Hank's or Viaspan®, which is available over-the-counter at a drugstore. The coach and all medical personnel at a speed skating competition should be alert to the importance of knowing how to care for a knocked-out tooth.

Fractures and Broken Bones

It is sometimes difficult to distinguish a broken finger from one that is merely jammed. Use a cold pack to control swelling and pain. If there is no improvement within the hour, the finger should be X-rayed.

To safely move a person with an injury to the hand or wrist, follow these steps:

- A finger with a mild swelling can be taped to an adjacent finger.
- An elastic bandage may be gently wrapped around an injured wrist to give the wrist support. Do not wrap heavily, and do not pull the bandage tight.

A fracture or a broken bone can be recognized by some or all of the following:

- A part of the body is bent or twisted out of its normal shape.
- A bone has pierced the skin.
- Swelling is severe and more than the swelling associated with a typical sprain or bruise.
- The hand or foot becomes extremely cold, which may indicate pinching of a major blood vessel.

If the speed skater has a possible broken leg or arm, the best approach is *not* to move the leg or arm in any manner. A cold pack can be used to lessen the discomfort until medical personnel arrive, and the skater should be kept warm with a blanket. It is important to get prompt medical attention when a fracture occurs.

Remember: *Never* move a seriously injured speed skater. Instead, get prompt medical attention or call for emergency aid. Until medical personnel arrive, cover the injured skater with a lightweight blanket, to reduce the risk of shock.

10

Great Names in Speed Skating History

Speed skating has provided the Olympics with some of its most memorable moments and performers. Through the 1998 Games, 200 different individuals—134 men and 66 women—had won Olympic medals in long-track skating. Today's fans may not be aware of the contributions and colorful stories of athletes of years gone by.

Jeanne Ashworth (USA)

Instead of building a bobsled run, organizers of the 1960 Olympics in Squaw Valley, California, added women's speed skating to the Games. There were four events on the schedule, and the U.S got a medal in the very first one.

Jeanne Ashworth (born July 1, 1938) claimed that first medal, a bronze at 500 meters, to lead the showing by the six-member American women's team. Four years later, she tied for fourth place in the 500. Over her career, Jeanne, from Wilmington, New Jersey, collected 14 National and North American indoor and outdoor championships, and set 10 U.S. indoor records.

Cy White / PHOTO ACTION USA

Bonnie Blair

Bonnie Blair (USA)

Bonnie Blair was destined to be a speed skater, it seems. When she was about to be born, on March 18, 1964, her father was on his way to a competition with two of Bonnie's siblings. So he dropped her mother off at the hospital and later heard of Bonnie's birth on the public address system at the rink. Bonnie's family had her on skates by the age of two in their hometown of Champaign, Illinois.

Bonnie's great talent became apparent when, at the age of 19, she placed eighth in the 500 meters at the 1984 Olympics in Sarajevo. She continued her climb up the international ranks over the next four years and provided the "Blair Bunch" with one of its biggest thrills at the Calgary Olympics. Bonnie's gold medal in the 500 meters came in world-record time, and she also won a bronze in the 1,000 and placed fourth in the 1,500.

By winning gold in the 500 and 1,000 at both the 1992 Albertville Olympics and the 1994 Lillehammer Games, Bonnie became America's most decorated female Olympian, Winter or Summer. "I love what I'm doing," Bonnie said in 1995 as her career was winding down. "When you have that strong a passion, you give everything you have."

The winner of three World Sprint Championships, Bonnie has also received numerous honors, including the Amateur Athletic Union's Sullivan Award in 1992, *Sports Illustrated* magazine's 1994 Sportswoman of the Year, and the US Olympic Committee/ Associated Press 1994 Athlete of the Year.

Since her retirement, Bonnie has been a member of the board of US Speedskating and has served in numerous fundraising roles for speed skating and the USOC. Bonnie also has worked as a television commentator for speed skating events. In addition, she helped coach her husband, David Cruikshank, to a spot on the 1998 Olympic team. Bonnie and David are the parents of a son, Grant, born in July 1998, and a daughter, Blair, born in July 2000.

Gaetan Boucher (Canada)

One might think that Canada, with its cold northern climate, has always been a speed skating power. But the country went through a long dry spell in Olympic speed skating between 1952 and 1980, a period during which Canada won just one medal, a silver by Cathy Priestner in the 500 in 1976. For the men, it was Gaetan Boucher who revived Canada's fortunes by winning medals in the 1980 and '84 Winter Games.

Gaetan was born on May 10, 1958, in Charlesbourg, Quebec, the fourth of six children. His father wanted him to play hockey, but he gravitated to the new speed skating club in Sainte-Foy, the suburb of Quebec City where the family lived. Today, the rink there bears his name.

In his early teens, Gaetan began to devote himself to speed skating, and in 1973 he became the youngest member of the national team. At his first World Sprints in 1975, Gaetan finished last in the 34-man field. That didn't discourage Gaetan. He set to work to improve himself for the 1976 Olympics, and at Innsbruck he placed sixth in the 1,000 meters.

As impressive as that breakthrough was, it didn't compare to what Gaetan accomplished in 1980. At that year's Lake Placid Olympics, Gaetan started out with an eighth-place performance in the 500 meters. In the 1,000 a few days later, Gaetan had the good fortune to be paired with Eric Heiden. That bit of luck provided Gaetan with a great pacesetter, and Gaetan's time proved fast enough for the silver medal. Later that season, on the tight turns of a hockey rink, Gaetan won the world short-track title with victories in three of the four distances.

Over the next few years, Gaetan focused on long-track skating. In early 1983, while practicing at a hockey rink, he went skidding into the boards and shattered his left ankle. Could he possibly recover in time for the 1984 Olympics? Gaetan answered all the doubters with the best season of his life. He was the star of the Sarajevo Games, winning bronze in the 500 and golds in the 1,000 and 1,500.

Gaetan was the toast of Canada for having won that country's first-ever Olympic speed skating gold medal. In fact, he was Canada's only speed skating Olympic champion until Catriona Le May Doan won the 500 in Nagano. He also won the 1984 World Sprints, making him the only man to have won world titles in both long- and short-track skating.

In 1985, Gaetan's ankle started acting up again, and he finished a shocking 15th in the World Sprints in Sainte-Foy. He began special therapy on his ankle in March 1987 and decided to try a comeback for the Calgary Olympics. Gaetan skated well in the 1,000 meters, placing fifth. The 1,500 would be his final Olympic race, and Canadian fans roared their approval as he skated near gold-medal pace for most of the way. On his last lap, however, Gaetan faded, and he ended up ninth. Still, he was proud of himself. "I'm not so disappointed with my result," Gaetan said. "I've had four Olympic Games. A lot of people dream of competing in one."

Eric Flaim (USA)

Eric Flaim has one of the most fascinating résumés in speed skating history. A native of Pembroke, Massachusetts, Eric was born on March 9, 1967, and competed in his first Olympics in 1988. He finished fourth in the 5,000- and 1,000-meter races, before skating to a silver in the 1,500. On the final day of the Olympics, he came up with another fourth-place performance in the 10,000. His versatility was apparent, and one week later, Eric won the World Allround Championship.

Back problems beset Eric in the early '90s, and at the Albertville Games in 1992 he was slowed in his three races by a case of food poisoning. Still, he managed to place sixth in the 5,000 meters. By 1993, Eric had switched back to short-track skating (he had been national champion in 1983 and 1985), and he qualified for the '94 Olympic squad. With Eric skating the anchor leg in Lillehammer, the Americans won the silver medal in the 5,000-meter relay, still (as of 2001) the only medal by the U.S. men in Olympic short-track history. It's the medal of which Eric said he was most proud.

Eric retired in 1994 to operate a successful inline skating store in Boston, but was lured back to the U.S. team for the 1998 Olympics. Eric was selected by the captains of the American teams in all sports at Nagano to be the U.S. flag bearer at the opening ceremony. On the ice, Eric helped the Americans place sixth in the 5,000-meter relay. Since Nagano, Eric has pursued a variety of business interests, including short-track commentary for NBC Sports.

Eric Heiden and Beth Heiden (USA)

Jack and Nancy Heiden instilled a love of sports in their children, so it wasn't surprising that little Eric and Beth hardly ever sat still. What did surprise people, years later, was what great athletes they had become. In fact, some say Eric and Beth Heiden grew up to be two of the best ever.

Eric and Beth, from Madison, Wisconsin, achieved most of their fame at the 1980 Olympic Winter Games. Eric won all five men's speed skating events, and Beth claimed a bronze. But their success wasn't limited to those two memorable weeks in Lake Placid, New York. Over his career, Eric won two World Junior Championships, four World Sprint Championships, and three World Allround Championships. Beth was a World Junior champion and to this day remains the only American woman to win the World Allround title.

Eric was born on June 14, 1958, and Beth on September 27, 1959. Their dad had been captain of the fencing team in college and continued to participate in sports. Their mom was a skilled skater, a city tennis champion, and a swimmer. Eric first got on skates at age two, helped by his grandfather Thomsen, a former ice hockey coach at the University of Wisconsin. As a kid, Eric loved to play hockey and soccer. Beth, meanwhile, became a national record holder in the mile run, was ranked No. 1 on her school tennis team, and competed in swimming and diving. Throughout this period, Eric and Beth were moving up the ranks in speed skating, and they began training seriously when Eric was 14 and Beth 13.

With Dianne Holum coaching them, Eric and Beth began to see great improvements. Both skated in the 1976 Olympics at Innsbruck, Austria. One of their most amazing seasons was 1976–77, when Eric was a high school senior and Beth was a junior. Eric won the first of his two straight World Junior Championships, the first of his three consecutive World Allround titles, and the first of his four-in-a-row World Sprints crowns.

Before that, no American had ever won the World Allround title, signifying the best skater who races both sprints and long distances. No man from the United States had ever been World Sprints champion until then, either. And no skater from any country had ever won all three World Championships in a single year. Beth, meanwhile, opened some eyes by placing fourth at the women's World Allround meet.

The year before the Lake Placid Games gave the Heidens another chance to make history. Both Eric and Beth were World Allround champions, winning all four races that comprise the meet. Besides setting a meet record for points, Beth also became the first U.S. woman to win the Allround title.

No wonder expectations were so high when the Heidens arrived for the 1980 Olympics. Eric rose to the challenge, though not all of his five gold medals came easily. He had a close call in the 1,500 meters, the middle-distance race that pits sprint stars against those who usually skate the longest events. About midway through the race, on a turn, Eric slipped when his left skate got caught in a rut in the ice. For a nervous moment, it looked as if he would fall. But he regained his rhythm quickly and won his fourth gold.

Another dramatic win came in the final event, the 10,000 meters. Eric spent the evening before the race at the U.S.-Soviet hockey game, where two of his childhood friends from Madison, Mark Johnson and Bob Suter, were playing. With all the excitement of the American hockey team's upset victory, Eric had trouble falling asleep, and he overslept by more than an hour the next day. Somehow, Eric settled into a strong pace and won the race in world-record time.

For Beth, the Lake Placid Games proved far more difficult. For one thing, she had a sore ankle at the Olympics. For another, reporters who weren't familiar with the world of speed skating assumed that Beth would be as dominant in her events as Eric was in his. Beth did perform fairly well, placing seventh in the

1,500- and 500-meter races and fifth in the 1,000. But with each race in which she didn't win a medal, Beth faced questions about what some considered a subpar showing. Finally, in the last women's event, Beth skated a solid third-place time and collected a bronze medal.

After they left speed skating, both Eric and Beth became world-class cyclists—Eric even raced in the famous Tour de France. Beth also was a member of the University of Vermont's NCAA champion ski team. Away from sports, Beth earned a degree in structural engineering, and Eric followed in his father's footsteps and became an orthopedic surgeon. Recently, Eric has helped the U.S. speed skating team's medical staff at several meets.

When he made his great breakthrough to the top of the speed skating world, Eric said, "All the time I was looking up to those guys, those Russians and Scandinavians, saying how good they were, and suddenly it's me!" More than 20 years after their fabulous achievements, skating fans still look up to Eric and Beth Heiden.

Anne Henning (USA)

Anne, born on September 6, 1955, helped spark a wave of interest in speed skating in her hometown of Northbrook, Illinois, a Chicago suburb that's barely an hour from the 400-meter oval in Milwaukee. In fact, the Northbrook Speed Skating Club has been represented on every U.S. Olympic speed skating team since 1960.

Anne started skating in 1964. Just three years later she was the national champion in the midget age group (11 and under). She switched from short-track skating in 1970, and the following year she set world records in the 500 and 1,000 meters. Also in 1971, Anne became the first U.S. woman to medal in the World Sprint Championships, taking golds in both 500-meter events (both in world-record time) and the overall silver.

At the 1972 Sapporo Olympics, Anne, just 16 years old, won the 500-meter gold in a most unusual way. She already had posted an Olympic-record time of 43.73 seconds when it was ruled she had been impeded by the skater she was paired with as they changed lanes. Given a second opportunity to race at the end of the competition, Henning, skating solo, went even faster; she was the only skater all day under 44 seconds. She also won the 1,000-meter Olympic bronze medal to wrap up a remarkable career.

Dianne Holum (USA)

From her days as a 16-year-old Olympic medalist to the memorable years she coached her daughter to international awards and records, Dianne Holum (born on May 19, 1951) was a major figure in American speed skating. In 1968, at Grenoble, France, Dianne was part of the unprecedented three-way tie for the silver medal in the 500 meters and captured the bronze in the 1,000. She then returned to her high school studies in Northbrook, Illinois, and looked forward to the '72 Olympics.

At Sapporo, Dianne was selected as the first woman to be the U.S. flag bearer for the Winter Games opening ceremony. In the competition, her strong finishing laps gave her gold in the 1,500 (the first ever by a U.S. woman) and silver in the 3,000. That also gave her a unique double distinction: winner of every color of Olympic medal, and winner of an Olympic medal at every distance available to women. "It was a thrill to see the [American] flag," Dianne said following one of her 1972 medal ceremonies.

Dianne was a member of seven world teams and twice won overall bronze medals at the World Allround Championships. Just 20 years old when she retired from elite competition, Dianne turned her attention to college at the University of Wisconsin. While in Madison, a couple of young skaters caught her eye—the brother-sister duo of Eric and Beth Heiden. Dianne became their coach and helped them skate to Olympic glory at Lake Placid in 1980. A student of Dutch training methods, Dianne also coached Dan Jansen, Bonnie Blair, and Sweden's four-time Olympic medalist Tomas Gustafson early in their careers.

When the Winter Games returned to Japan in 1998, Dianne Holum was on the ice once again, this time coaching her daughter, Kirstin Holum, who was born on June 29, 1980. Kirstin, who had won the 1997 World Junior Championship, continued Dianne's tradition of excellence with two top-seven finishes and a pair of world junior records. As the Games concluded, Dianne and Kirstin Holum announced their retirements from coaching and skating, ending one of the great chapters in U.S. Olympic history.

Dan Jansen (USA)

Dan Jansen's victory in the 1,000 meters at the 1994 Lillehammer Olympics will be remembered as one of the most dramatic moments in Winter Games history. The favorite and world record holder entering the 500-meter competition four days earlier, Dan slipped in the last turn and had to reach for the ice with his left

Cy White / PHOTO ACTION USA

Dan Jansen skates with younger athletes at
Pettit National Ice Center in Milwaukee.

hand. That bobble cost him precious hundredths of a second, and his time was only the eighth-fastest of the day. Dan felt he'd let people down. "Sorry, Milwaukee," he said to a reporter from his hometown. Fortunately, a sports psychologist had been helping Dan recognize his opportunity in the 1,000 meters. For months, Dan had been writing "I love the 1,000" on notes to himself. When race day came, Dan found himself both relaxed and energized. His time of 1 minute, 12.43 seconds was a world record and nearly three-tenths of a second ahead of the field.

Dan, the youngest of nine children, was born on June 17, 1965, and began skating when he was four years old. Besides skating, he also excelled at baseball and football. For a long time, Dan struggled to keep up with his brother Mike's pace. But by 1984, Dan was the best in his family and one of the best in the world. He was just 18 when he placed a promising fourth in the 500 at the Sarajevo Olympics. A week before the 1988 Calgary Games, he dominated the World Sprint Championships. Sadly, however, the morning of his first Olympic race in Calgary, Dan's sister Jane died after a courageous battle with leukemia. Dan fell in that race and in the 1,000 meters later in the Games.

It seemed that 1992 would bring Dan his Olympic medal, but the weight of expectations and poor ice conditions not suited to his powerful style left him empty-handed. Then came the letdown in the 500 at the Lillehammer Games. It all added up to a very satisfying feeling when Dan finally won his gold in the 1,000. "I was thankful all the pressure was over, thankful my family could stop living this Olympic nightmare and feeling sorry for me," Dan wrote in his autobiography *Full Circle*.

Dan's many awards included the Olympic Spirit Award in 1988 and the USOC's male Athlete of the Year and the AAU's Sullivan Award in 1994. He also set eight world records and won two World Championships and dozens of World Cup medals. Dan's triumph after years of disappointment have made him a sought-after motivational speaker since his retirement from skating in 1994.

Charlie Jewtraw (USA)

By winning the 500-meter race at the 1924 Olympics, "Chick" Jewtraw became America's very first Winter Olympics gold medalist and the only U.S. champion at the Games in Chamonix, France. Jewtraw's strength was his explosive start. His starting split of 100 yards was once timed at 9.4 seconds, an astonishing pace given the skates and ice conditions of the day. Born on May 5, 1900, Jewtraw grew up skating in Lake Placid, New York, and his international fame greatly contributed to his hometown's reputation as a winter sports playground. He lived to the age of 95. His gold medal is housed at the Smithsonian Institution in Washington, DC.

Karin Kania, Christa Luding, and Andrea Ehrig (East Germany)

East Germany was a dominant sports power in the 1970s and 1980s, and its female speed skaters were a fearsome team. Three of the very best were Karin (Enke, Busch) Kania, Andrea (Mitscherlich, Schone) Ehrig, and Christa (Rothenburger) Luding, all from the prominent sports club in Dresden, about 100 miles south of Berlin. Combined, they won 18 Olympic medals and dozens of World Championship and World Cup medals.

Shortly before the 1980 Olympics opened, 18-year-old Karin, a former competitive figure skater, was considered no better than an alternate on the East German speed skating team. Then she won the World Sprints title—the first of six she would collect over her career. Karin (born June 20, 1961, in Dresden) went on to take gold in the 500 meters at Lake Placid; she added a silver in 1984 and a bronze in 1988 in that event. In 1,000-meter Olympic races, she captured a gold in 1984 and a silver in '88. She also won the 1,500-meter title in 1984 at Sarajevo and placed second in that distance in Calgary. This remarkable athlete's range went all the way to 3,000 meters, where she was the silver medalist in 1984 and skated a courageous race in 1988 before placing fourth. "She's a big girl with long legs. She's just made for the sport," U.S. skater Nancy Swider-Peltz once said. Karin's eight Winter Olympic medals in individual events broke a record that had stood since 1936. Her total was surpassed in 1998, when Norwegian skier Bjorn Dahlie captured three to bring his total to nine individual medals.

Andrea, who was born December 1, 1960, in Dresden, enjoyed a long career, skating in four Olympics starting with the 1976 Games in Innsbruck, when she was just 15 years old. By winning the silver in the 3,000 meters in 1976, she became the youngest medalist in an Olympic individual event—a record still standing 25 years later. Andrea was a member of the East German team in 1980, but her best result that year was fourth in the 3,000. She was back in top form for Sarajevo, winning the gold in the 3,000 in Olympic-record time, plus silvers in the 1,000 and 1,500. Two more silvers came her way in 1988, in the 3,000 and the new event for women, the grueling 5,000 meters.

Christa, born December 4, 1959, in Weisswasser, was a great two-sport athlete. She won the gold medal in the 500 meters at the 1984 Olympics, and before the next Games she was a world champion in both speed skating and bicycling. She became a friendly rival of Bonnie Blair and finished second to Bonnie by just two one-hundredths of a second in the 500 at Calgary. In the 1,000 that year, Christa captured the gold, Karin Kania the silver, and Bonnie Blair the bronze. Later in 1988, Christa became the only athlete to win medals in Winter and Summer Games in the same year by taking silver in track cycling's sprint race in Seoul, South Korea.

Germany was reunified in 1990, ending the era of the East German sports machine. After reunification, Christa Luding made one last Winter Olympics appearance in 1992, picking up a bronze in the 500, with Bonnie Blair winning once again. While German women have continued to enjoy success in the past few years, chances are slim that fans will soon see a trio like Karin Kania, Andrea Ehrig, and Christa Luding.

Johann Olav Koss (Norway)

Many Olympic medalists hope to use their status as star athletes to bring them wealth. But amassing personal riches has taken a back seat to helping the less fortunate for Norway's great champion Johann Olav Koss.

Johann began to write his Olympic legend at the 1992 Albertville Games. The day of the opening ceremony, Johann was hospitalized in Bavaria with an inflamed pancreas. His recovery was not only swift but complete. Five days later, he was racing in the Olympic 5,000 meters (he placed seventh), and two days after that he earned the gold in the 1,500.

A similar story line played out in 1994. Johann struggled early in the season and had a knee problem. But when the gun fired at the Olympics, he set his sights on nothing short of victory. He began a memorable Games with a victory in the 5,000 meters, earning him a meeting with King Harald. The 1,500, three days later, brought him a second gold. After that race, Johann announced he would donate his entire bonus (225,000 kroner, or about $32,000) to Olympic Aid, a relief program for the children of war-ravaged Sarajevo, site of the 1984 Winter Games, and the East African region of Eritrea. Johann also urged Norwegians to give 10 kroner (about $1.43) for every gold medal their nation won at the Games. "It is important that we show solidarity with people who don't have it as good as we have it here inside the Viking Ship," he explained.

In winning the 10,000 meters, he broke the world record by an astonishing 12.99 seconds; his margin of victory (almost 19 seconds) was second-greatest in Olympic speed skating history. He became the first Olympian in history to win three golds all with world-record times.

Johann used his fame as a platform to speak out on behalf of impoverished and physically challenged children all around the world. After retiring from competition, he helped create Olympic Aid Atlanta, which worked with UNICEF in relief efforts and reached an estimated 15 million children in 15 countries. Together, Johann's Atlanta and Lillehammer Olympic Aid programs raised $27.5 million.

Johann was named Sportsman of the Year by *Sports Illustrated* in 1994 (the magazine also honored Bonnie Blair that year) and has received many other honors for his sports and humanitarian efforts. His contributions to sports include serving on several anti-doping commissions, and working to promote winter sports in Australia. In 1999 he became a full member of the International Olympic Committee.

The son of two doctors, Johann was studying medicine at the time of the 1998 Games when all three of his Olympic records were erased. The generosity and goodwill exhibited by Johann Olav Koss, however, will never fade.

Peter Mueller and Leah Poulos Mueller (USA)

When many couples become engaged, they start choosing gold-edged wedding invitations and silverware patterns. Not Peter Mueller and Leah Poulos. Just after they decided to get married, Peter and Leah began collecting gold and silver Olympic medals. At the 1976 Games, Peter, from Madison, Wisconsin, made history by winning the first-ever 1,000-meter men's gold medal. His fiancée, from the skating-rich community of Northbrook, Illinois, grabbed the silver in the women's 1,000.

The Olympic victory by Peter (born July 27, 1954) was one of his most amazing wins ever. Because of nerves and a flu epidemic in the Olympic Village, he had hardly eaten for two weeks before his first race. However, he placed an encouraging fifth in the 500 meters. The next day he won his 1,000-meter race by more than a second, the first Olympic speed skating gold by an American man since 1964. Peter's recovery was short-lived, however. That evening he began running a high fever, and the following day he was permitted out of bed only long enough to attend his own medal presentation; he had to scratch from that day's 1,500 meters.

Meanwhile, Leah (born October 5, 1951) had the misfortune of skating in the same Olympics as Soviet great Tatiana Averina. Tatiana was one of the Games' most versatile and talented skaters. The women's competition began with the 1,500 meters, with Tatiana earning the bronze medal and Leah finishing sixth. Then came the 500, and Tatiana collected her second bronze, just four one-hundredths of a second ahead of Leah. Finally, Leah's best event arrived—the 1,000 meters. Again Tatiana beat her, but she was the only skater who could make that claim that day. Leah's silver-medal time was just 0.14 second behind Tatiana's Olympic-record victory.

By 1980, Peter and Leah were married. Peter handed Eric Heiden a rare defeat at the final Olympic Trials race in the 1,000 meters. But a few weeks later, at the Lake Placid Games, Peter's best effort was good enough only for fifth place. Leah, meanwhile, won silver medals at both 500 and 1,000 meters, losing only to women turning in Olympic-record times.

"She was a much better skater than I was. I just got lucky," Peter once said. Years later, Peter was lucky enough to coach Dan Jansen to his famous 1,000-meter victory at the Lillehammer Olympics, a result Peter said made him happier than his own gold-medal performance. In 1998, Peter added to his incredible résumé when he directed the Dutch Olympic sprinters to four medals. Today, he coaches a private team in the Netherlands that includes distance star Gianni Romme. For several years, Leah served as an administrator with the U.S. speed skating team.

Ard Schenk (Netherlands)

Adrianus "Ard" Schenk began his Olympic career quietly enough, placing 13th in the 1,500 meters at the 1964 Innsbruck Games. By the time he retired, Ard was one of speed skating's all-time stars, and his accomplishments were celebrated throughout the Netherlands. In fact, he was so revered that a variety of tulip was named for him.

Ard was born on September 16, 1944, the son of a former national speed skating coach. He began international competition in 1964 and just two years later won the first of his three European Championships.

Ard had talked of retirement after winning only a silver medal, in the 1,500, in the 1968 Grenoble Olympics. He not only continued skating, he also continued improving. By 1972, while also studying to be a physical therapist, he held three speed skating world records.

He opened the competition at the Sapporo Games by winning the 5,000 with a bit of luck. Ard competed in the first pair of the day, and during his race it began to snow heavily at the Makomanai Ice Rink. Thus, Ard was finished skating before conditions got even more challenging. The following day brought the 500 meters, an event known to be Ard's weakest. Still, the fans were shocked when he stumbled at the start and fell after just four steps. It took just one day, however, for Ard to regain his form. He won the 1,500 meters in an Olympic record, and the day after that he added the 10,000-meter gold with a strong opening 4,000 meters.

Two weeks later, Ard swept the four-event World Championship, the first skater to achieve that feat in 60 years.

Ard gave up his amateur status to skate on a short-lived professional circuit in 1973, then retired from competition. He has served in an administrative position as the Dutch speed skating team's *chef de mission* at the Winter Olympics, and as a member of the International Skating Union's five-member speed skating technical committee. The National Olympic Committee of the Netherlands awarded him its Medal of Honor in 1998.

Dutch skaters have maintained the high standard Ard set for them. In the 26 years following Ard's triple-gold performance, the Dutch claimed 45 Olympic medals, including 11 by the 1998 squad.

John Shea and Irving Jaffee (USA)

At the 1932 Games, Lake Placid's own John "Jack" Shea (born September 10, 1910) captured the 500- and 1,500-meter gold medals, and Irving Jaffee (born 1906) won the 5,000 and 10,000. Years later, also at Lake Placid, Eric Heiden matched their feat of sweeping all the men's races for the United States.

Irving had started skating at the age of 16 with mail-order skates that were four sizes too big. His mother had been hoping he could "grow into them," so Irving dutifully stuffed newspaper into the toes and wore several pairs of socks. His race results were forgettable. Finally, he borrowed a pair of skates that fit and began to win medals. Irving was an early practitioner of office training, such as calisthenics, cycling, running, and weight work—components of every modern speed skater's regimen.

After riding in the post-Olympic parade down Fifth Avenue in New York City, Irving endured a series of disappointments. He had no job to return to, so he pawned his Olympic golds and some 400 other medals for $2,000. In the year he had to repay the loan, the Depression worsened and the pawnshop was torn down to make way for a skyscraper. Irving's treasures were gone. "Hero today, gone tomorrow," he once mused.

Jack, meanwhile, could have contended for medals at the 1936 Garmisch-Partenkirchen Games in Germany, but he decided not to attend, in protest against Adolf Hitler's Nazi regime. His son James competed in three Nordic events at the 1960 Squaw Valley Games, and his grandson Jim was a top candidate for the 2002 Games in the new Olympic sledding sport called skeleton. Jack has remained active in speed skating for decades, including appearing in 2001, at age 90, at a fundraiser for the U.S. team.

Lydia Skoblikova (USSR)

Years before Eric Heiden, a Soviet skater earned the distinction of sweeping all the events on the Olympic schedule. Her name was

Lydia Skoblikova (born March 8, 1939), and she achieved her remarkable feat at the 1964 Winter Games in Innsbruck, Austria.

Until 1960, no official speed skating events for women were included on the Olympic schedule. But at the '60 Games, in Squaw Valley, California, Lydia, then a 20-year-old physiology student from Chelyabinsk in the Ural Mountains of Russia, set to work showing what female athletes could do. She began those Games by winning the 1,500 meters in a world-record time. The following day, she placed fourth in the 1,000 meters. And two days after that, she won the 3,000 meters, at that time the longest speed skating event offered to women.

By the time the Innsbruck Games rolled around, Lydia was working as a teacher and was the reigning World Allround champion, having swept all four races at that meet. Lydia won her first two races—the 500 and 1,500 meters—in Olympic-record time. Then, in the 1,000, she not only set an Olympic record, she also made Olympic history. That win made her the first woman ever to win three golds in a single Games and the first athlete ever to capture five Olympic championships. She completed her sweep and won her sixth career Olympic gold medal by taking the 3,000, some 3.5 seconds ahead of the runner-up.

At Innsbruck, according to Olympic historian David Wallechinsky, Lydia wore a good-luck pin given to her by the wife of a U.S. coach. When American skater Terry McDermott heard about this, he too asked his coach's wife for a pin and shocked the experts by winning the 500-meter gold medal.

Lydia's six golds were the most Winter Olympic victories in any sport until Bjorn Dahlie of Norway won three in skiing in 1998, raising his gold medal total to eight. No matter how you rank her among the all-time greats, Lydia Skoblikova surely set the standard for the women speed skaters who came after her. No woman has matched her clean sweep of the Olympic medals, and with skaters now specializing in either sprints or longer distances, none is likely to do so.

Cathy Turner (USA)

Cathy Turner is one of the most amazing athletes in all of Olympic speed skating. Not only is she the most-decorated American in short-track history, with four Olympic medals, but she also has one of the most inspirational stories to tell.

Cathy was born on April 10, 1962, and grew up in Rochester, New York. She seemed to be on her way to making the long-track speed skating team for the 1980 Olympics in nearby Lake Placid (short-track wasn't on the Olympic schedule yet). She certainly had worked hard enough, driven to excel since the age of six by a very demanding father. But Cathy missed out on the team, and she quickly struck out on her own to pursue a musical career under the name Nikki Newland.

Cy White / PHOTO ACTION USA

Cathy Turner, two-time Olympic gold medalist,
checks the alignment of her skates for any imperfections.

For nearly nine years, Cathy battled severe clinical depression and an identity crisis. Then, in 1988, she realized that she would be happiest as a skater, not a singer/songwriter, and returned to the ice. The difference this time would be that she would be competing to fulfill *her* dreams, not her father's.

Cathy was 29 years old when short-track skating made its official Olympic debut at the 1992 Albertville Games. Just two events were offered for women, and Cathy made the most of them. She helped the U.S. team to a silver medal in the 3,000-meter relay, and two days after that she skated in the 500 meters. Cathy advanced through the preliminary rounds to the final, then seemed headed for disaster when she clicked skates with another competitor in the closing meters. But Cathy regained her balance and stretched her foot across the line to win in a photo finish.

Those heroics brought fame and new opportunities to Cathy. She won numerous awards and was President George H.W. Bush's guest at a White House state dinner. She even learned to figure skate so she could perform with the Ice Capades show. Because of the change in the scheduling of the Olympics, however, the Lillehammer Games were coming up soon, and Cathy resumed her short-track training.

Cathy arrived in Norway with hopes of three medals, as the 1,000 meters had been added to the women's lineup. She took the first step toward that goal by skating on the bronze-medal team in the 3,000-meter relay. Two days later, Cathy skated three controversial races in the 500 meters. In both the quarterfinals and semifinals, top skaters got tangled up with Turner and were eliminated from the competition. Cathy advanced to the final, and in the late going made a gutsy pass on the outside to take the lead from the world record holder. A second 500-meter gold medal belonged to Cathy, but by now she also was the owner of a reputation as a dirty skater. When the 1,000 meters was contested two days after the 500, Cathy was disqualified for an illegal pass in the semifinal round.

Though she would be nearly 36 years old at the time of the Nagano Games, Cathy was ready to put herself to the test once again. She was able to win a spot on the U.S. team for the 3,000 relay, and helped the team make it to the semifinals, but there the Americans were eliminated. Winning the "B" final earned the U.S. squad fifth place and gave Cathy Turner the opportunity to put things into perspective. "I have to go in there and tell the girls, 'Hey. we're here in the Olympics,' " she told reporters in Nagano. "That's cool all by itself."

Sheila Young (USA)

Here's an athlete who liked to do things in threes. She won a gold medal at 500 meters, silver in the 1,500, and bronze in the 1,000 at the 1976 Olympics. She captured three World Sprint Championships, and she showed her versatility by also winning three world cycling championships.

Sheila, born October 14, 1950, grew up in Detroit, one of four children. Her mother died when Sheila was 13, and Sheila's dad Clair, who had been a speed skater himself, knew the sport was an activity the family could enjoy together.

When Sheila was 21, she narrowly missed the bronze medal in the 500 meters at the 1972 Olympics. By the time Innsbruck rolled around, she was on the cover of *Sports Illustrated* and on top of her game. In fact, she might well have done even better than her bronze-medal finish in the 1,000 meters if she had had better skating conditions. When the ice was resurfaced partway through that competition, too much water was applied on the track at the Ice Stadium, and Sheila was unable to improve on the earlier skaters' times.

Still, Sheila became the first-ever U.S. athlete to win three medals in a single Winter Games. Another first happened one day at the Olympic Village, when President Gerald Ford phoned his congratulations—making Sheila the first U.S. gold medalist to receive such a call. After her remarkable performance in 1976, the *International Herald Tribune*, a newspaper published in Paris, called Sheila a greater athlete than even the celebrated Babe Didrikson.

Sheila's three medals helped the U.S. team to 10 overall in the 1976 Games, the Americans' best showing in 16 years. And it raised the standard toward which U.S. athletes aspire. Today, Sheila and her husband Jim Ochowicz cheer for their daughter Elli Ochowicz (born December 15, 1983). Elli was, at age 14, the youngest competitor at the 1998 long-track speed skating Olympic Trials. Elli placed second in the 2001 Junior National Championships and was considered a strong candidate for the 2002 Olympic team.

11

Speed Skating Records

Like any Olympic sport governed by a stopwatch, speed skating keeps many records. The lists have undergone almost constant changes since 1987, when the first enclosed 400-meter oval came into service, and again since 1997, when clap skates became popular.

In track, there's one set of records for outdoor events (on a 400-meter surface) and another for indoor competition, where the size of the running surface can vary widely. Swimming keeps records for short-course pools (25 yards) and long-course pools (50 meters). In long-track speed skating, though, skating 400 meters is skating 400 meters, whether it's on a windswept day outdoors in Lake Placid, New York, or in the climate-controlled comfort of the Utah Olympic Oval. Many fine performances continue to be seen at the open-air ovals in Inzell, Germany, and Davos, Switzerland. However, heading into the 2001–02 season, all but three of the 157 recognized world, American, junior world, junior American, Olympic, World Allround, World Sprints, and World Single Distance records were set indoors.

Yet another argument can be made about races skated at high altitudes, which are known to have beneficial effects in sprint competition. For years, record seekers made the long trip to

Alma-Ata (some 2,300 miles southeast of Moscow) to race at its 5,500-foot-high Medeo oval. Nowadays, skaters set their sights on more accessible facilities. In 2000–01, 24 world records were set at either Calgary (elevation 3,400 feet) or Salt Lake City (elevation 4,675 feet). The thin air at high altitudes is a physiological detriment to distance skaters, however. The 5,000-meter women's and 10,000-meter men's records fell in November 2000 at Heerenveen, Netherlands (elevation just 1 foot above sea level).

While some skating aficionados think a separate record list should be maintained for outdoor races and perhaps also for high-altitude results, for now at least, the International Skating Union endorses just a single set of official records.

As detailed in Chapter 3, besides the records for individual events, there are records for combined races. These scores come in three types: the rarely contested allround short samalog (500, 1,000, 1,500, and 3,000 meters); allround long samalog, used in the World Allround Championships; and the sprint samalog, used in the World Sprint Championships. Individual races for which there are world records, but very limited competition, are the women's 10,000 meters and the men's 3,000.

Abbreviations of ISU Member Countries

In results and record lists, countries are identified by three-letter abbreviations. Bear in mind that not every member nation of the International Skating Union participates in speed skating; some are involved only in figure skating. ISU national abbreviations are as follows:

Andorra (AND)

Armenia (ARM)

Australia (AUS)

Austria (AUT)

Azerbaijan (AZE)

Belarus (BLR)

Belgium (BEL)

Bosnia-Herzegovina (BIH)

Bulgaria (BUL)

Canada (CAN)

China (CHN)

Chinese Taipei (TPE)

Croatia (CRO)

Cyprus (CYP)

Czech Republic (CZE)

Denmark (DEN)

Estonia (EST)

Finland (FIN)

France (FRA)

Georgia (GEO)

Germany (GER)

Great Britain (GRB)

Greece (GRE)

Hong Kong (HKG)

Hungary (HUN)

Iceland (ISL)

Israel (ISR)

Italy (ITA)

Japan (JPN)

Kazakhstan (KAZ)

Korea, Democratic People's Republic of (North) (PRK)

Korea, Republic of (South) (KOR)

Latvia (LAT)

Lithuania (LTU)

Luxembourg (LUX)

Mexico (MEX)

Mongolia (MGL)

Netherlands (NED)

New Zealand (NZL)

Norway (NOR)

Poland (POL)

Portugal (POR)

Romania (ROM)

Russia (RUS)

Slovak Republic (SVK)

Slovenia (SLO)

South Africa (RSA)

Spain (ESP)

Sweden (SWE)

Switzerland (SUI)

Thailand (THA)

Turkey (TUR)

Ukraine (UKR)

United States (USA)

Uzbekistan (UZB)

Yugoslavia (YUG)

Long Track Records

LADIES' RECORDS

500 meters

World
Catriona Le May Doan (CAN)   37.29   Salt Lake City 3/9/01

American
Chris Witty (USA)   38.36   Salt Lake City 3/9/01

Jr. World
Sayuri Osuga (JPN)   38.58   Calgary   1/29/00

Jr. American
Elli Ochowicz (USA)   39.26   Calgary   3/17/00

Olympic
Catriona Le May Doan (CAN) 38.21   Nagano   2/14/98

Olympic (Tot.)
Catriona Le May Doan (CAN) 76.60   Nagano   2/13/98
                                                (38.39/38.21)   2/14/98

World Allrounds
Chris Witty (USA)   39.45   Heerenveen   3/13/98

World Single Distance
Catriona Le May Doan (CAN) 37.29   Salt Lake City 3/9/01

World Single Distance (Tot.)
Catriona Le May Doan (CAN) 74.72   Salt Lake City 3/9/01
                                                (37.43/37.29)

World Sprints
Catriona Le May Doan (CAN) 37.86   Calgary   2/21/99

1,000 meters

World
Monique Garbrecht (GER)   1:14.13 Salt Lake City 3/10/01

American
Chris Witty (USA)   1:14.58 Calgary   3/3/01

Jr. World
Heike Hartmann (GER)   1:16.92 Calgary   3/3/01

Jr. American
Sarah Elliott (USA)   1:18.78 Calgary   3/17/01

Olympic
Marianne Timmer (NED)   1:16.51 Nagano   2/19/98

World Single Distance
Monique Garbrecht (GER)   1:14.13 Salt Lake City 3/10/01

World Sprints
Monique Garbrecht (GER)   1:14.61 Calgary   2/21/99

1,500 meters

World
Anni Friesinger (GER)   1:54.58 Salt Lake City 3/10/01

American
Jennifer Rodriguez (USA)   1:55.30 Calgary   3/4/01

Jr. World
Sarah Elliott (USA)   1:59.24 Calgary   3/16/01

Jr. American
Sarah Elliott (USA)   1:59.24 Calgary   3/16/01

Olympic
Marianne Timmer (NED)   1:57.58 Nagano   2/16/98

World Allrounds
Annamarie Thomas (NED)   1:56.96 Hamar, NOR   2/7/99

World Single Distance
Anni Friesinger (GER)   1:54.58 Salt Lake City 3/10/01

3,000 meters

World
Claudia Pechstein (GER)	3:59.26 Calgary	3/2/01

American
Jennifer Rodriguez (USA)	4:06.59 Calgary	3/2/01

Jr. World
Song Li (CHN)	4:10.30 Calgary	1/30/00

Jr. American
Catherine Raney (USA)	4:11.83 Calgary	3/27/98

Olympic
Gunda Niemann-Stirnemann (GER)	4:07.29 Nagano	2/11/98

World Allrounds
Gunda-Niemann-Stirnemann (GER)	4:02.01 Hamar, NOR	2/6/99

World Single Distance
Gunda Niemann-Stirnemann (GER)	4:00.34 Salt Lake City	3/9/01

5,000 meters

World
Gunda Niemann-Stirnemann (GER)	6:52.44 Salt Lake City	3/10/01

American
Kirstin Holum (USA)	7:14.20 Nagano	2/20/98

Jr. World
Kirstin Holum (USA)	7:14.20 Nagano	2/20/98

Jr. American
Kirstin Holum (USA)	7:14.20 Nagano	2/20/98

Olympic
Claudia Pechstein (GER)	6:59.61 Nagano	2/20/98

World Allrounds
Gunda Niemann-   6:57.24   Hamar, NOR 2/7/99
Stirnemann (GER)

World Single Distance
Gunda Niemann-   6:52.44   Salt Lake City 3/10/01
Stirnemann (GER)

10,000 meters

American
Nancy Swider-Peltz   17:37.35 Savalen, NOR 3/16/80

Short Samalog

World
Cindy Klassen (CAN)   155.576   Calgary   3/15-17/01

American
Becky Sundstrom (USA) 161.439   Calgary   11/27-29/98

Jr. World
Wieteke Cramer (NED) 162.452   Calgary   3/17-18/00

Jr. American
Sarah Shapiro (USA)   166.512   Calgary   3/20-21/99

Long Samalog

World
Gunda Niemann-   161.479 Hamar, NOR 2/6-7/99
Stirnemann (GER)

American
Jennifer Rodriguez   166.022 Hamar, NOR 2/6-7/99
(USA)

Jr. American
Kristin Holum (USA)   172.927 Milwaukee   2/21-22/96

World Allrounds
Gunda Niemann-   161.479   Hamar, NOR   2/6-7/99
Stirnemann (GER)

Sprint Samalog

World
Catriona Le   150.085   Calgary   1/6-7/01
May Doan (CAN)

American
Chris Witty (USA)   152.905   Calgary   2/20-21/99

Jr. World
Sayuri Osuga (JPN)   155.565   Calgary   3/18-19/00

Jr. American
Elli Ochowicz (USA)   159.221   Calgary   3/17-18/00

World Sprints
Monique Garbrecht   151.605   Calgary   2/20-21/99
(GER)

Source: http://www.usspeedskating.org/records/
LadiesLongTrackRecords.html

MEN'S RECORDS
500 meters

World
Hiroyasu Shimizu (JPN)   34.32   Salt Lake City 3/10/01

American
Casey FitzRandolph (USA) 34.72   Salt Lake City 3/10/01

Jr. World
Masaaki Kobayashi (JPN)   35.93   Calgary   3/19/00

Jr. American
Cory Carpenter (USA)   37.07   Calgary   3/8/96

Olympic
Hiroyasu Shimizu (JPN)   35.59   Nagano   2/10/98

Olympic (Tot.)
Hiroyasu Shimizu (JPN)   71.35   Nagano   2/9-10/98
                          (35.76/35.59)

World Allrounds
Jae-Bong Choi (KOR)   36.01   Milwaukee   2/5/00

World Sprints
Jeremy Wotherspoon   34.76   Calgary   2/21/99
(CAN)

World Single Distance
Hiroyasu Shimizu (JPN)   34.32   Salt Lake City 3/10/01

World Single Distance (Tot.)
Hiroyasu Shimizu (JPN)   68.96   Salt Lake City 3/10/01
                          (34.64/34.32)

1,000 meters

World
Jeremy Wotherspoon   1:08.28   Salt Lake City   3/11/01
(CAN)

American
Casey FitzRandolph   1:08.62   Calgary   3/2/01
(USA)

Jr. World
Masaaki Kobayashi (JPN) 1:10.83   Calgary   3/18/00

Jr. American
Eric Krantz (USA)   1:13.49   Calgary   3/18/00

Olympic
Ids Postma (NED)   1:10.64   Nagano   2/15/98

World Sprints
Jan Bos (NED)   1:08.55   Calgary   2/21/99

World Single Distance
Jeremy Wotherspoon   1:08.28   Salt Lake City   3/11/01
(CAN)

1,500 meters

World
Kyu-Hyuk Lee (KOR)   1:45.20   Calgary   3/15/01

American
Derek Parra (USA)   1:46.20   Salt Lake City   3/9/01

Jr. World
Shingo Doi (JPN)   1:47.33   Calgary   3/17/01

Jr. American
Ron Macky (USA)   1:50.67   Calgary   11/27/99

Olympic
Adne Sondral (NOR)   1:47.87   Nagano   2/12/98

World Allrounds
Adne Sondral (NOR)   1:47.01   Hamar, Norway 2/7/99

World Single Distance
Adne Sondral (NOR)   1:46.10   Salt Lake City   3/10/01

3,000 meters

World
Gianni Romme (NED)   3:42.75   Calgary   8/11/00

American
Jondon Trevena (USA)   3:49.68   Calgary   3/17/00

Jr. World
Mark Tuitert (NED)   3:48.56   Calgary   3/19/99

Jr. American
Ron Macky (USA)   3:51.43   Calgary   11/26/99

5,000 meters

World
Gianni Romme (NED)   6:18.72   Calgary   1/30/00

American
KC Boutiette (USA)   6:31.75   Calgary   3/2/01

Jr. World
Johan Rojler (SWE)   6:31.10   Calgary   3/17/01

Jr. American
Ron Macky (USA)   6:49.73   Calgary   11/28/99

Olympic
Gianni Romme (NED)   6:22.20   Nagano   2/8/98

World Allrounds
Gianni Romme (NED)   6:26.14   Milwaukee   2/5/00

World Single Distance
Bob de Jong (NED)   6:19.58   Salt Lake City   3/9/01

10,000 meters

World

Gianni Romme (NED)	13:03.40	Heerenveen, Netherlands	11/26/00

American

KC Boutiette (USA)	13:44.03	Nagano	2/17/98

Jr. American

Nick Pearson (USA)	14:25.81	Milwaukee	1/10/99

Olympic

Gianni Romme (NED)	13:15.33	Nagano	2/17/98

World Allrounds

Gianni Romme (NED)	13:23.94	Milwaukee	2/6/00

World Single Distance

Gianni Romme (NED)	13:08.71	Calgary	3/29/98

Mini Samalog

Jr. American

Mike Kagen (USA)	157.422	Calgary	11/26-28/99

Short Samalog

World

Erben Wennemars (NED)	149.188	Calgary	8/14-15/99

American

Joey Cheek (USA)	152.179	Calgary	11/26-28/99

Jr. World

Shingo Doi (JPN)	151.258	Calgary	3/15-17/01

Jr. American

Ron Macky (USA)	154.574	Calgary	11/26-28/99

Long Samalog

World

Rintje Ritsma (NED)	152.651	Hamar, Norway	2/6-7/99

American

Derek Parra (USA)	154.009	Calgary	1/14-16/00

Jr. American

Ron Macky (USA)	164.394	Milwaukee	12/17-18/99

World Allrounds

Rintje Ritsma (NED)	152.651	Hamar, Norway	2/6-7/99

Sprint Samalog

World

Jeremy Wotherspoon (CAN)	138.310	Calgary	2/20-21/99

American

Casey FitzRandolph (USA)	141.530	Calgary	2/20-21/99

Jr. World

Masaaki Kobayashi (JPN)	143.015	Calgary	3/18-19/00

Jr. American

Eric Krantz (USA)	149.005	Calgary	3/17-18/00

World Sprints

Jeremy Wotherspoon (CAN)	138.310	Calgary	2/20-21/99

Source: http://www.usspeedskating.org/records/
MensLongTrackRecords.html

Junior Records

Junior records can be set by skaters 18 years and younger. The skater cannot have reached the age of 19 by July 1 preceding the competition. Additionally, the United States breaks down its junior category into three age groups: Junior A (ages 17–18), Junior B (ages 15–16) and Junior C (14 and younger). Except for Junior C boys who wish to petition into a Junior B event, athletes cannot "skate up" a division. American junior records for both male and female skaters can be found on the US Speedskating web site: http://www.usspeedskating.org/records/Recordsintro.html.

Short Track Records

Short-track records are less meaningful than long-track records, since short-trackers race directly against one another instead of against the clock. Another difference between the two forms of competition is that short-track facilities and equipment have changed little in the last 20 years. Just four world records were set in the 2000–01 season.

LADIES' RECORDS

500 meters

World
Evgenia Radanova (BUL)   43.873   Lake Placid, N.Y.   2/18/00

Olympic
Isabelle Charest (CAN)   44.991   Nagano   2/29/98

American
Amy Peterson (USA)   44.844   Szekesfehervar,   11/8/98
Hungary

Jr. World
Marie-Eve Drolet (CAN)   45.305   Warsaw   1/6/01

Jr. American
Caroline Hallisey (USA)   45.900   Lake Placid, N.Y.   2/18/00

1,000 meters

World
Yang Yang (A) (CHN)   1:31.991 Nagano   2/21/98

Olympic
Yang Yang (A) (CHN)   1:31.991 Nagano   2/21/98

American
Amy Peterson (USA)   1:33.530 Nagano   2/21/98

Jr. World
Moon-Jung Kim (KOR)   1:32.702 Montreal   1/17/99

Jr. American
Julie Goskowicz (USA)   1:34.01   Beijing   1/11/97

1,500 meters

World
Moon-Jung Kim (KOR)   2:21.844 Montreal   1/17/99

American
Amy Peterson (USA)   2:25.168 Szekesfehervar, 11/7/98
Hungary

Jr. World
Moon-Jung Kim (KOR)   2:21.844 Montreal   1/17/99

Jr. American
Julie Goskowicz (USA)   2:30.55   Marquette,   1/11/97
Mich.

3,000 meters

World
Eun-Kyung Choi (KOR)   5:01.976 Calgary   10/22/00

American
Amy Peterson (USA)   5:05.362 Bormio, Italy 3/27/98

Jr. American
Julie Goskowicz (USA)   5:08.66   Marquette,   12/15/96
                                    Mich.

3,000-meter Relay

World
Korea   4:16.260 Nagano   1/17/98
(Sang-Mi An, Lee-Kyung Chun, Yun-Mi Kim, Hye-Kyung Won)

Olympic
Korea   4:16.260 Nagano   1/17/98
(Sang-Mi An, Lee-Kyung Chun, Yun-Mi Kim, Hye-Kyung Won)

American   4:21.875 Lake Placid, N.Y. 2/17/00
Julie Goskowicz, Caroline Hallisey, Sarah Lang, Amy Peterson

Source: http://www.usspeedskating.org/records/
LadiesShortTrackRecords.html

MEN'S RECORDS
500 meters

World
Jeffrey Scholten (CAN)   41.742   Calgary   3/4/00

Olympic
Takafumi Nishitani (JPN)   42.756   Nagano   2/21/98

American
Apolo Anton Ohno (USA)   41.916   Calgary   10/21/00

Jr. World
Francois-Louis   42.568   Montreal   1/16/99
Tremblay (CAN)

Jr. American
Apolo Anton Ohno (USA)   41.916   Calgary   10/21/00

1,000 meters

World
Jeffrey Scholten (CAN)   1:26.970   Calgary   3/5/00

Olympic
Satoru Terao (JPN)   1:29.398   Nagano   2/17/98

American
Apolo Anton Ohno (USA)   1:27.410   Chang Chun,   12/5/99
                                                    China

Jr. World
Seung-Jae Lee (KOR)   1:28.220   Warsaw,   1/7/01
                                                    Poland

Jr. American
Apolo Anton Ohno (USA)   1:27.410   Chang Chun,   12/5/99
                                                    China

1,500 meters

World
Eric Bedard (CAN)   2:15.393   Edmonton 3/3/01

American
Apolo Anton Ohno (USA)   2:15.977   Calgary   10/20/00

Jr. World
Misi Toth (USA)   2:17.146   Bay City,   12/17/00
                                                    Mich.

Jr. American
Apolo Anton Ohno (USA)   2:15.977   Calgary   10/20/00

3,000 meters

World
Dong-Sung Kim (KOR) 4:46.727 Szekesfehervar, 11/8/98
Hungary

American
J.P. Shilling (USA) 4:50.60 Marquette, Mich. 12/3/95

Jr. World
n/a n/a n/a n/a

Jr. American
Apolo Anton Ohno 4:51.147 Szekesfehervar, 11/8/98
(USA) Hungary

5,000-meter Relay

World
Korea 6:49.618 Chang Chun, China 12/5/99

Olympic
Japan 7:01.660 Nagano 2/21/98

American 7:02.014 Nagano 2/21/98
Eric Flaim, Andy Gabel, Tom O'Hare, Rusty Smith

Source: http://www.usspeedskating.org/records/
MensShortTrackRecords.html

Additional Olympic Records

Most Total Medals
Ladies Long Track

(tie) Karin (Enke, Busch) Kania (East Germany) and Gunda (Kleemann) Niemann-Stirnemann (East Germany, Germany), 8

Men's Long Track

(tie) * A. Clas Thunberg (Finland) and Ivar Ballangrud (Norway), 7

Ladies Short Track

(tie) Cathy Turner (USA) and Chun Lee-kyung (South Korea), 4

Men's Short Track

(tie) Chae Ji-hoon (South Korea) and Kim Ki-Hoon (South Korea), 3

* Includes the four-race overall championship, conducted only in 1924

Most Gold Medals
Ladies Long Track

Lydia Skoblikova (USSR), 6

Men's Long Track

(tie) * A. Clas Thunberg (Finland) and Eric Heiden (USA), 5

Ladies Short Track

Chun Lee-kyung (South Korea), 4

Men's Short Track
Kim Ki-Hoon (South Korea), 3

* Includes the four-race overall championship, conducted only in 1924

Most Silver Medals

Ladies Long Track

Andrea (Mitscherlich, Schone) Ehrig (East Germany), 5

Men's Long Track

Kees Verkerk (Netherlands), 3

Ladies Short Track

Yang Yang (S) (China), 3

Men's Short Track

Frederic Blackburn (Canada), 2

Most Bronze Medals

Ladies Long Track

Natalia Petruseva (Soviet Union), 3

Men's Long Track

Roald Larsen (Norway), 4

Ladies Short Track

Amy Peterson (USA), 2

Men's Short Track

Many with 1

Largest Margin of Victory

Men's Long Track

24.8 seconds, Hjalmar Andersen (Norway), 10,000 meters, 1952

Ladies Long Track

6.53 seconds, Christina Baas-Kaiser (Netherlands), 3,000 meters, 1972

Men's Short Track

.700 seconds, Canada, 5,000-meter relay, 1998

Ladies Short Track

5.4 seconds, South Korea, 3,000-meter relay, 1994

Smallest Margin of Victory

Men's Long Track

.02 seconds, Tomas Gustafson (Sweden), 5,000 meters, 1984

Note: The 500 meters in 1928 was a first-place tie.

Ladies Long Track

(tie) .02, Bonnie Blair (USA), 500 meters, 1988, and Blair, 1,000 meters, 1992

Men's Short Track

.02, Chae Ji-hoon (South Korea), 500 meters, 1994

Ladies Short Track

.04, Cathy Turner (USA), 500 meters, 1992

12

For Further Reading and Reference

While speed skating is a relatively small sport, there's no shortage of reading materials available to fans and competitors. The author recommends these:

BOOKS

For Young Readers

Arnold, Caroline. *The Olympic Winter Games.* Franklin Watts, 1991.

Blair, Bonnie, with Greg Brown. *Bonnie Blair: A Winning Edge.* Taylor Publishing, 1996.

Breitenbucher, Cathy. *Bonnie Blair: Golden Streak.* Lerner Publications, 1994.

Brimmer, Larry Dane. *Speed Skating.* Children's Press, 1997.

Olympic Games

Chamonix to Lillehammer: The Glory of the Olympic Winter Games. United States Olympic Committee, 1994. This is one of several oversize commemorative books licensed by the USOC. When the Winter and Summer Games were held in the same year, the books carried the names of the host cities, such as *Barcelona Albertville 1992.* Earlier editions were titled simply *United States Olympic Book.* All offer contemporary accounts of the competitions. I've located several from 20 or more years ago at used bookstores. Check out the bad 1970s hairstyles.

Wallechinsky, David. *The Complete Book of the Winter Olympics.* Overlook Press, 1997. Nowhere else will you find eight-deep results for every Olympic race ever contested. Wallechinsky updates his outstanding book with each Olympics.

Speed Skating

Fox, Mary Virginia. *The Skating Heidens.* Enslow Publishers, 1981. This book portrays two remarkable athletes and gives insight into the popularity of speed skating in Europe.

Holum, Dianne. *The Complete Handbook of Speed Skating.* Enslow Publishers, 1984. Eric Heiden's training log is one of the interesting elements of this instructive, highly technical book. Recommended only for the advanced skater or coach.

Jansen, Dan, with Jack McCallum. *Full Circle.* Villard Books, 1994. DJ recounts his long and sometimes heartbreaking career.

Publow, Barry. *Speed on Skates.* Human Kinetics Publishers, 1999. This is one of the most up-to-date and comprehensive books available; plenty of technical and training information.

Speedskating Handbook 2000-2001, Amateur Speedskating Union of the United States, 2000. Chock-full of requirements for organizing and running a meet, plus brief bios of the more than

100 members of the ASU Hall of Fame. Also includes contact information for 19 state and regional skating associations. Send a $5 check to:

> ASU
> OS 651 Forest
> Winfield, IL 60190.

Magazines

Fitness and Speed Skating Times brings together technical information, results, and features on ice and inline speed skating. Eight issues per year, plus an online edition.

> Fitness and Speed Skating Times
> 2401 NE 15th Terrace
> Pompano Beach, FL 33064
> phone: (954) 782-5928
> fax: (954) 782-1044
> Internet: http://www.speedsk8in.com
> e-mail: speedsk8in@aol.com

Speedskating World, an English-language magazine published in the Netherlands, is great for those seeking timely, extensive results of international competitions. Eight issues per year.

> Speedskating World
> Redactiebureau Irene P.
> Floris van Lijndestraat 8
> 4041 GP Kesteren The Netherlands
> phone: (+31) 488 48 26 95
> fax: (+31) 488 48 36 95
> Internet: http://www.speedskatingworld.com
> e-mail: irenep@wnet.bos.nl

Newsletters

Ice Chips is US Speedskating's newsletter, including technical information, schedules, and information of interest to clubs and associations. It is available both as a printed newsletter and online. Published about five times a year. For information, go to: http://www.usspeedskating.org/.

The Racing Blade is published five times a year by the Amateur Speedskating Union. Emphasis is on information helpful to the grassroots skater, coach, parent or official. For information, go to: http://www.speedskating.org/.

Web Sites

The ISU's web site offers links to a some 900 speed skating-related sites. See: http://www.isu.org/links/.

When using the Google search engine to research specific skaters, I found dozens of sites, newspaper articles, and other items of interest. Some sites are authorized by leading skaters, such as www.caseyfitz.com, for the American speed skater Casey FitzRandolph.

The Netherlands—a nation two-thirds the size of West Virginia, but with a whopping 16 400-meter skating ovals—is home to the sport's most rabid followers and statistics nuts. What is perhaps skating's most comprehensive fan web site comes from Holland. Not all links are in English. Check out: http://www.gironet.nl/home/cvstaave/.

Another outstanding site is www.speedskating.com. It offers news, event results, equipment information and advertising, and more. Go to: http://www.speedskating.com/.

NBC holds the U.S. television broadcast rights for the Olympics (both Winter and Summer) through 2008. Its Olympics-specific web site is: http://www.NBCOlympics.com/.

Newspaper sites

While nearly every newspaper in the country carries Olympic news during the Games, several papers offer outstanding coverage of speed skating and the Olympic movement on a continuing basis. Among the best are:

Atlanta Journal-Constitution
http://www.accessatlanta.com/partners/ajc

Boston Globe
http://www.boston.com

Chicago Tribune
http://chicagotribune.com

Deseret News, Salt Lake City
http://deseretnews.com

Los Angeles Times
http://www.latimes.com

USA Today
http://www.usatoday.com/olympics/oly.htm

13

Glossary

ASU Amateur Speedskating Union of the United States, the association that has governed grassroots and recreation-level speed skating for all ages. This organization planned to merge with US Speedskating effective in March 2000.

Blade covers Fabric covers used to absorb moisture from skate blades.

Blade guards Plastic or leather protectors used to prevent damage to skate blades.

Clap skates Speed skates with movable blades attached to the bottom of the boot with a system of hinges and springs. As the blade snaps back into place at the end of each skating stroke, it produces a "clap" sound.

Crossover The type of step needed to negotiate a turn. The right foot crosses over the left so the athlete skates the shortest distance possible.

Also refers to the area on the backstretch of a 400-meter oval where skaters switch lanes each lap to equalize the overall distance.

Dry-land Training conducted off the ice, such as weightlifting, cycling, or running.

Forward swing The movement of the arm in front of the skater.

Glide Using the momentum of the push to move forward while on support leg.

Helmet A required protective device for short-track skaters. Also highly recommended for cross-training on a bicycle or inline skates.

Ice-sledge A sled equipped with skating-style blades, permitting disabled athletes to race in events similar to wheelchair competitions.

Inline skating A popular dry-land training activity. Speed skaters use five-wheel skates.

Inner The inside lane of the two lanes used for metric-style competition on a 400-meter oval.

ISU International Skating Union. The governing body that sanctions world competition, including the Olympic Games, in both short- and long-track racing.

Jig A rack used to hold skate blades securely for sharpening.

Knee pads Required safety equipment for short-track skaters.

Lap One full trip around a skating track. In long-track skating, a lap is 400 meters; in short-track skating, 111 meters.

Long track Competition taking place on a 400-meter oval, with athletes racing two at a time against the clock.

Low walk A specific dry-land training technique. A skater assumes the skating position and walks, either on a flat surface or uphill.

Metric *See* **Long track.**

Opener A long-track skater's first split time. In the 500 meters, for instance, the first 100 meters is the opener.

Outer The outside lane of the two lanes used for metric-style competition on a 400-meter oval.

Oval A long-track skating rink, usually 400 meters.

Pack-style Competition involving a group of skaters who compete directly against one another.

Pair Two skaters who race against one another and against the clock in a long-track competition.

Personal best A personal record time. Skaters keep track of their best times in each distance and at specific rinks. Also called a *personal.*

Plyometric jumps Dry-land exercises in which a skater hops into the air and pulls his knees up to his chest. Such exercises can improve a skater's explosiveness from the starting line and thus are especially important to sprint specialists.

Push   Using the skate to propel the skater forward.

Pushing leg   The leg that is pushing to the side in the skating stroke.

Rear swing   The swing of the arm behind the skater.

Samalog   The scoring system used in elite-level long-track competition. Times are converted to points, with the lowest point total winning.

Shin guards   Equipment that protects a short-track skater from injuries when inadvertently kicked by another skater.

Short track   Competition on a 111-meter track, usually laid out on a standard hockey rink.

Sit   The basic body position for all types of speed skating. The skater bends the knees 90 to 100 degrees and bends at the waist, as though sitting in a chair but hunched forward.

Skin   A synthetic, one-piece skating suit, with or without an attached hood.

Split   The time for a portion of a skating race, such as for a 400-meter segment of a long-track event.

Stone   A hand-held device used to sharpen the skate and blade and to smooth away imperfections in a skate blade.

Stroking   The combination of pushing and gliding used in speed skating

Support leg   The leg supporting the skater's weight.

US Speedskating   The recognized U.S. national governing body of speed skating for world and Olympic competition, merging with the ASU in March 2002.

Weight shifting   Transferring a skater's weight to the support leg during the skating stroke.

14

Olympic and Speed Skating Organizations

The organization of, and participation in, the Olympic Games requires the cooperation of a number of independent organizations.

The International Olympic Committee (IOC)

The IOC is responsible for determining where the Games will be held. It is also the obligation of its membership to uphold the principles of the Olympic Ideal and Philosophy beyond any personal, religious, national, or political interest. The IOC is responsible for sustaining the Olympic Movement.

The members of the IOC are individuals who act as the IOC's representatives in their respective countries, not as delegates of their countries within the IOC. The members meet once a year at the IOC Session. They retire at the end of the calendar year in which they turn 70 years old, unless they were elected before the opening of the 110th Session (December 11, 1999). In that case, they must retire at the age of 80. Members elected before

1966 are members for life. The IOC chooses and elects its members from among such persons as its nominations committee considers qualified. There are currently 113 members and 19 honorary members.

The International Olympic Committee's address is—

Chateau de Vidy
Case Postale 356
1007 Lausanne, Switzerland
phone: (+41) 21 621 61 11
fax: (+41) 21 621 6216
Internet: http://www.olympic.org

The National Olympic Committees

Olympic Committees have been created, with the design and objectives of the IOC, to prepare national teams to participate in the Olympic Games. Among the tasks of these committees is to promote the Olympic Movement and its principles at the national level.

The national committees work closely with the IOC in all aspects related to the Games. They are also responsible for applying the rules concerning eligibility of athletes for the Games. Today there are more than 150 national committees throughout the world.

The U.S. Olympic Committee's address is—

One Olympic Plaza
Colorado Springs, CO 80909-5760
phone: (719) 632-5551
fax: (719) 578-4654
Internet: http://www.usolympicteam.com

Speed Skating Organizations

US Speedskating
PO Box 450639
Westlake, OH 44145
phone: (440) 899-0128
fax: (440) 899-0109
Internet: http://www.usspeedskating.org/
e-mail: usskate@ix.netcom.com

Amateur Speedskating Union of the United States (ASU)
OS 651 Forest St.
Winfield, IL 60190-1541
phone: (800) 634-4766 or (630) 784-8662
fax: (630) 784-8667
Internet: http://www.speedskating.org/
e-mail: ASUkostal@aol.com

International Skating Union (ISU)
Chemin de Primerose 2
CH 1007
Lausanne, Switzerland
phone: (+41) 21 612 66 66
fax: (+41) 21 612 66 77
Internet: http://www.isu.org/
e-mail: info@isu.ch